THE BLOOD'S DECREE

ENDORSEMENTS

In his new book, *The Blood's Decree*, author, pastor, and revivalist Jim Cernero reveals an amazing and mysterious truth found in Scripture in the book of Hebrews—that the blood of Yeshua, Jesus Christ speaks supernaturally! It decrees! (Hebrews 12:24) I encourage all who read it to discover the "better things" that Jesus' blood speaks over you today!

Sid Roth

Internationally known host of *It's Supernatural!*

The Cross of Jesus was not a sanitary, gilt icon but rather the method of a gory execution—where His precious blood was spilled for us. Jim Cernero presents a fascinating look at the powerful blood of Jesus, uncovers forgotten history, dispels myths, and offers applications that can change your life!

Tim Enloe

Conference Speaker/Author

www.timenloe.com

This timely book is a reminder of the transformative truth found in the blood of Jesus. Jim Cernero writes with deep conviction, biblical insight, and a passion for helping believers grasp the fullness of Christ's finished work. Whether you are a new Christian or a seasoned follower of Christ, you will be stirred to greater faith, deeper worship, and renewed confidence in God's power to save, heal, and deliver. This message is more than theology, it's victory, freedom, and hope. I wholeheartedly recommend this book to anyone longing to walk in the full power of the Cross.

Tiff Shuttlesworth
Founder, Lost Lamb Association
President, Northpoint Bible College & Seminary

I will never forget the first time I was taught about the power in the blood of Jesus. A woman told me to begin praying the power of the blood of Jesus over my life and over all of the addictions and shackles that kept me bound. I boldly began praying, "The blood of Jesus covers me and has freed me from these chains!" That prayer began to break open the prison doors I had lived in all my life. *The Blood's Decree* is a gift to our generation, and the Lord has given Pastor Jim the revelation of freedom, restoration, and healing found only in the blood of Jesus. The enemy has attempted to conceal this truth from God's Word because he knows the power to overcome is held in *the Blood's decree!* May this book ignite faith in your spirit and awaken your heart as you boldly declare the power that the blood of Jesus speaks!

Cristina Baker
Author and Cofounder, Power of Hope Ministries

If you've never truly understood the weight that the blood of Jesus holds, Pastor James will take you on a journey of true revelation that will forever change your walk with Christ! Once we grasp this revelation, we will live in spiritual confidence every single day knowing the blood of Jesus speaks, protects, and reveals truth. There's power in the blood!

Jordan and Kelsey Morris
Founders, All For Jesus Evangelistic Ministry

THE BLOOD'S DECREE

RECEIVE THE DIVINE HEALING, PROTECTION, AND BLESSING THAT JESUS' BLOOD SPEAKS OVER YOU

JIM CERNERO

 All emphasis within Scripture quotations is the author's own. Take note that the name satan and related names are not capitalized. We choose not to acknowledge him, even to the point of violating grammatical rules.

DESTINY IMAGE® PUBLISHERS, INC.
P.O. Box 310, Shippensburg, PA 17257-0310
"Publishing cutting-edge prophetic resources to supernaturally empower the body of Christ"

This book and all other Destiny Image and Destiny Image Fiction books are available at Christian bookstores and distributors worldwide.

For more information on foreign distributors, call 717-532-3040.
Reach us on the Internet: www.destinyimage.com.

ISBN 13 TP: 979-8-8815-0280-5
ISBN 13 eBook: 979-8-8815-0281-2
Hardcover: 979-8-8815-0283-6
Large Print: 979-8-8815-0284-3

For Worldwide Distribution, Printed in the U.S.A.
1 2 3 4 5 6 7 8 / 29 28 27 26 25

DEDICATION

First and foremost, I dedicate this book to my Lord and Savior Jesus Christ. I have been blessed to have known You since I was a young child, and Your presence in my heart and life is truthfully indescribable, incomparable, and a priceless treasure. You have, as David says in Psalm 3, been *"my Glory and the Lifter of my head"* through the mountaintop and valleys experiences of my life and journey of faith. Always my constant Companion by Your Holy Spirit, at times my Healer, Deliverer, and always my Provider, Protector, Enabler, and so much more.

I could never have imagined as a young boy who surrendered his life to You, Jesus, at the age of 9, how you would take me around the world many times over to minister for You with the musical and vocal talents you placed within me—and with the opportunity to preach Your Word, minister in the gift of healing to thousands, and see them come to the knowledge of salvation as a revivalist. Thank You for loving me and choosing me to be a minister of the gospel and for placing whatever gifts I have in me to use for Your glory.

To my amazing, beautiful wife of 40 years, Mindy! You are the love of my life! You have stood by me through the ups and downs of life and ministry, and I cannot thank the Lord enough for giving me the honor to have you as my wife and my partner for life. You are beautiful inside and out and God has gifted you with tremendous wisdom and insight that has been a source of strength throughout our marriage. I love you, Babe!

To our wonderful son, Daniel James Cernero. Words cannot express the joy I felt when the Lord woke me up from a sound sleep at 2:30 a.m. on December 1987 and I heard Him say in my spirit, "You're going to have a son." Tears of gratitude flooded my cheeks as I lay there praising God for His faithfulness to us as we had prayed for you for several years and now your birth was confirmed. From the moment we first held you in our arms, the love we feel for you is indescribable! You've always been such a blessing to your Mom and me. And now we love your beautiful wife, Linsey, too—she is precious to us.

To my parents who are now with the Lord, Nunziante and Rachel Cernero. I am eternally grateful to have had you as such godly parents! You both modeled faith and trust in God, taught us the Word of God, demonstrated your genuine relationship with the Lord and it is an immeasurable heritage that I cherish! I realize not everyone can claim that type of family faith heritage, and I don't take it lightly! Your unshakable trust in God helped forge my own deep and personal relationship and trust in God and has been a source of perpetual encouragement. I love and miss you and look forward to seeing you in Heaven!

To my brothers, Tom, Mark, John (my twin), and their sweet wives. I'm so blessed that you're my siblings! Tom and John, you are now enjoying the presence of the Lord in Heaven and are missed greatly here, but we are comforted knowing we have "the blessed hope" of being in the Lord's presence one day also. Much love!

To my precious and saintly grandparents on both sides of the family, my loving aunts and uncles and cousins, and all who know the Lord Jesus as their Savior, I'm so blessed that the Lord chose you to be my family and that we share a like faith in Christ that completes our bond. I love you all!

To my father-in-law and mother-in-law, Ron and Sandy Primrose. Thank you for raising a beautiful girl in the ways and knowledge of the Lord! Your impact and influence on Mindy played an important role in her maturing to be a strong woman of faith, an amazing wife, mother, and caring pastor's wife. Love you both!

ACKNOWLEDGMENTS

Larry Sparks, Publisher, Destiny Image. Thank you for the opportunity to publish this book and make it available for readers to be blessed by the Truth contained in its pages. Your zeal and passion for revival is so evident and a blessing to the body of Christ.

David Diga Hernandez. Thank you for writing the Foreword for this book, for your generosity to me, and for your friendship that is so very much appreciated. I'm so blessed to see how the Lord has anointed you and is using you to touch many for His Kingdom.

Pastor Benny Hinn. Your life of surrender and devotion to the Lord you adore has made an incalculable impact on millions and to me and my family. I'm honored to know you as my friend and brother in Christ!

To all the many pastors, professors, teachers, mentors, and the men and women of God who directly poured into my life and those who have ministered to me from afar, thank you for loving Jesus and surrendering your lives to make an impact for Christ on others like me.

To the prayer and financial supporters of Jim Cernero / Certain Sound Ministries, thank you from the bottom of our hearts for sowing into this ministry and helping to spread the saving, healing, and delivering power of God worldwide.

To our wonderful Certain Sound Church International family. Thank you for the love and support you've shown to me and Mindy! We are honored to be your pastors.

CONTENTS

FOREWORD

There is a powerful and undeniable theme woven throughout Scripture, a theme that speaks, that decrees, that testifies. It is the voice of the blood of Jesus, declaring redemption, righteousness, healing, deliverance, and eternal victory for every believer. In *The Blood's Decree,* my friend Jim Cernero masterfully unveils this truth, bringing the reader into a deeper revelation of what the blood of Jesus declares over our lives.

Each page calls you to listen, to receive, and to stand in agreement with what Heaven has already proclaimed. The blood of Jesus is not a distant historical concept. It is an ever-present, active, and powerful reality that continues to work in our lives today.

As you read, you will not only gain a greater understanding of the atoning work of Christ, but also find your faith stirred to walk in the fullness of what His blood has secured for you.

My prayer is that *The Blood's Decree* will ignite within you a fresh passion for the presence of God, a deeper love for Jesus, and a stronger confidence in the finished work of the Cross. May your heart resonate with the truth that the blood still speaks and what it speaks is life, power, and victory.

Let this book strengthen your faith, renew your mind, and draw you into a greater awareness of the limitless power of the blood of Jesus.

David Diga Hernandez
Evangelist

PREFACE

Scientific advancements in technology over the past few decades have now made it possible for the blood of an individual to *tell* examiners what is going on in someone's body. What malady that is unseen externally may be revealed through examining the blood of the individual, whether it be cancer, heart blockage, diabetes, and many other diseases. In a sense, the patient's blood *speaks* and indicates a potential health threat that needs to be addressed before it is too late to be reversed. On the positive side of things, a person's blood can also indicate that all levels are normal and that the patient is in good health and disease-free.

Criminologists now use advanced forensic methods on evidence left behind by the perpetrator of a crime to help determine who the person may be. Not that I have a morbid interest in death, but I enjoy watching shows that go through the process of how they utilize these methods to solve the crime. It's truly remarkable that now they can solve crimes that a few decades ago would have been relegated to "cold cases" as they didn't then have the tools they have now. These modern advances are even exonerating some who were falsely accused and spent years in prison for a crime they didn't commit.

Science has just in the last few years caught up with the Source of all knowledge, the Source of all Truth, God, who has known since the beginning of time that the blood speaks.

How amazing it is to know that the Bible, written centuries ago, has contained this truth all along—blood speaks. More significantly and profoundly, the blood of Jesus—the Son of God who was crucified on the Cross for our salvation and our healing—speaks! It decrees! (Hebrews 12:24)

INTRODUCTION

As early as I can remember, growing up in the late 1950s, '60s, and '70s, we frequently sang songs about the blood of Jesus and heard messages on the same in my home church in Nutley, New Jersey. Songs including "There's Power in the Blood," "There Is a Fountain Filled with Blood," "Oh the Blood of Jesus," "He Was Wounded for Our Transgressions" (and by His stripes we are healed), and more were sung often. It was clear even at my young age, that salvation is by the blood of Jesus, long before I knew the scriptural backing for this doctrinally.

I am blessed to have had a heritage in Christ on both sides of my family, both parents' parents having been saved and filled with the Holy Spirit. I was taught about the fact that not only did Jesus' blood pay for our salvation, but that same blood covers our hearts and lives as believers in Him and has tremendous power.

The blood of Jesus was (and is) central to our spiritual lives and was central to our belief system and faith. A common phrase used in prayer by my godly grandparents and my parents, was "Lord, *hover over them* and *cover them with Your blood, Jesus*" when praying over us, their children. It wasn't until years later that I became acutely aware of why they prayed that way and what happens when we do. More on that later.

In my teen years, the then-popular Christian artist Andre Crouch, authored and made popular the song "The Blood Will Never Lose Its Power," which was widely sung in the churches across the nation of all denominations. I distinctly recall, while visiting family members in Sherman, Texas, in 1971, hearing the pastor's wife, affectionately known as Aunt Mary Jo, sing with her powerful alto voice, "The blood that Jesus shed for me...way back on Calvary...." I will never forget the awesome presence of the Lord that I sensed in that moment that flooded my entire being. It's still a powerful song that brings home the reality of the power of Jesus' blood.

Many years later, while working in Nashville as a composer on songs for a new recording that my friend, the then well-known gospel tenor, Steve Brock, was about to record, Steve and the producer, Lari Goss, said to me, "Do you have any other songs we can include in the album?" I went back to my hotel room and thought about it, praying and meditating on the Word of God. Seeking inspiration from the Word of God, I opened my Bible to the book of Hebrews, chapter 10. This book of the Bible is an amazing thesis on the work of Jesus on the Cross, His office as our High Priest, and the *"new and living way"* He made for us to approach the throne of grace through the blood of Jesus.

Hebrews 10:19-20 (NKJV) declares to us, *"Therefore, brethren, having boldness to enter the Holiest by the blood of Jesus, by a new and living way which He consecrated for us, through veil, that is, His flesh."* Suddenly, I sensed the anointing come over me and the words of a song poured out of my spirit.

The song title that the Lord gave was "Through the Blood," and I will just give you the lyrics of the chorus which came as I meditated on this powerful declaration in Hebrews about what the blood of Jesus decrees over us:

It's through the blood of Christ I now can enter boldly
Into the presence of Jehovah God most holy
No other sacrifice could ever pay the pardon for my sin
Not by works of righteousness nor by deeds of earthly flesh
No other way to enter in but through the blood

I will never forget the awareness of the presence of the Lord that flooded my heart as these powerful words flowed from my pen! I believe wholeheartedly that when you mention, *speak* (decree), or sing about the blood of Jesus, whether in song or in a sermon or in prayer, there's an accompanying anointing and His presence becomes more real to you. By the grace of God, the song has been sung on Christian TV, in evangelistic crusades, and services around the world.

It seems, however, in more recent years there's been a shying away from mentions of the blood as if to say it's not politically correct to speak about and too controversial or perhaps gory and macabre. In my opinion, there's an intentional downplaying of the blood in preacher's sermons or messages, certain Bible translations, worship songs and choruses, and it's no doubt perpetrated by none other than the wicked one himself. He doesn't want believers to have a revelation of the power of the blood and it what it decrees to us.

Several of the newer translations of the Bible omit any reference to the words *blood, Cross, Calvary* altogether, and other words related to the subject. The current "woke movement," sadly, has infiltrated many churches and many pastors have succumbed to its deception. Perhaps unwittingly, they are acquiescing to this subtle ploy of the devil to de-emphasize, de-value, and disannul the power of the blood in their congregants and listeners, keeping God's people ignorant of its power, and held in bondage of all kinds.

There's Power in the Blood

This is a tragedy! There is no gospel without the blood of Jesus as Ephesians 1:7 (NKJV) declares, *"In Him we have redemption through His blood, the forgiveness of sins, according to the riches of His grace."* The blood of Jesus and what it speaks is essential to the gospel of Jesus Christ. To ignore mentions of the blood and its decrees is to forfeit its provisions. As the old, familiar gospel song says, "There's Power in The Blood." The enemy knows that and it's no surprise he doesn't want its power, its benefits declared or decreed in song or in messages from the pulpit.

This is nothing new. If you've studied church history, you know that during the second century there was a prevalent, heretical belief and movement that contradicted salvation through the blood of Jesus. Gnosticism is derived from the Greek word *gnosis,* which means knowledge. Stay with me here; there's a reason I am including this in *The Blood's Decree!*

In summary, the Gnostics believed salvation could be obtained through a special form of "secret knowledge." Adherents of this belief believed the material world was created by a lesser god, "Demiurge," and only through this special knowledge could a "divine spark" that resided in men be ignited causing spiritual enlightenment.

The early church fathers, such as Tertullian, Origen, Justin Martyr and others, condemned gnostic teachers and beliefs as heretical because it clashed with accepted Christian doctrine. One key belief of Gnosticism was the concept of dualism.

Gnostics believed that the world was divided into the physical and spiritual realms. The material world being evil and the spiritual world good. Their beliefs described God as incomprehensible and unknowable. This obviously conflicts with Christianity's concept of a personal God who desires relationship with human beings. John 3:16 (NKJV) clearly states, *"For so loved the world that He gave His only begotten Son, that whoever believes in Him should not perish but have everlasting life."*

The Gnostics believed that this inferior god was separate from the God of creation, from the God of redemption. The Word of God clearly tells us that Jesus was God in flesh in John 1:1-5 (NKJV):

> In the beginning was the Word [Jesus], and the Word was with God, and the Word was God. He was in the beginning with God. All things were made through Him, and without Him nothing was made that was made. In Him was life, and the life was the light of men. And the light [Jesus] shines in the darkness, and the darkness did not comprehend it.

When it comes to another key belief, regarding salvation Gnostics claimed that a "hidden knowledge" was the basis of salvation. This *secret revelation* frees the "divine spark" within humans, allowing only certain ones the opportunity to be saved and enter the realm of light.

They also believed that Jesus was not God in flesh. Rather, He was spirit who took on human form and appearance. These beliefs are at odds with the gospel that we Christians believe. Christianity teaches that salvation is available to everyone not just a special few and that it comes from grace through faith in Jesus Christ, not from study or works. Christians believe that the Bible is the only Source of Truth and that Jesus is very much God and was very much man.

The apostle John goes on to say in John 1:14 (NKJV), *"And the Word became flesh and dwelt among us, and we beheld His glory, the glory as of the only begotten of the Father, full of grace and truth."*

This truth is central to the gospel because if Jesus was just a spirit and had not taken on human form and become flesh and hadn't shed His blood, there could be no redemptive plan as spirits don't have blood. Moses testified prophetically, recorded in Hebrews 9, there would have been no way of salvation as there is no remission of sin without the shedding of blood. *"According to the law almost all things are purified with blood, and without shedding of blood there is no remission"* (Hebrews 9:22 NKJV).

The shedding of Christ's blood is central to our belief as Christians. Gnosticism nullifies the work of the Cross; it denies the deity of Christ and denies the shedding of Christ's blood that is essential to the work of salvation. If the blood wasn't shed, it would not have decreed salvation thereby paying the price for our redemption.

This devaluing, erasing the blood in many modern-day church preaching, literature, and music, is in my opinion a somewhat resurgence of this ancient Gnostic teaching. The New Age movement and the New Thought movements of our day use a lot of terms that sound good and seem to be in alignment with the gospel, but they are in fact dangerously at odds with the gospel and are based on heresies.

We need to be careful when hearing words including "enlightenment," "self-actualization," "your truth," and so on. These can often be pathways to error and lead away from *the Truth*. There's no "your truth" or "my truth"—there's only *the Truth*. Truth is found in Jesus, the Word! Jesus says in John 14:6 (NKJV), *"I am the way, the truth, and the life. No one comes to the Father except through Me."* Exactly contrary to the belief of the Gnostics! The only knowledge we need to be saved is the knowledge of the Lord! The knowledge and the truth that His blood speaks!

This was prophetically foreshadowed in the structure of the tabernacle in the wilderness. The three entrances of the tabernacle were called "The Way, The Truth, and the Life." This is why the Pharisees were so enraged when Jesus proclaimed He was such because to them the tabernacle was a sacred part of their religion and how dare He compare Himself to it! He still is the Way, the Truth, and the Life, and the only way to God is through His precious blood that speaks!

Is it any wonder that statistics tell us that many in the church are bound by addictions of various kinds, which includes preachers and pastors? The much-publicized moral failures of high-profile pastors and ministers, particularly those having succumbed to the allure of sexual temptation, may indeed be the result of satan accomplishing his plan to denigrate the power of the blood of Jesus to keep us from sin and deliver God's people from victory over the flesh. There is *still* power in the blood!

We cannot afford to allow this! We must be aware of what the blood decrees and speak it accordingly to push back the ploys of the enemy.

I believe the Holy Spirit has given me an insight to what the well-known, often quoted Scripture Revelation 12:11 (NKJV) means, which states: *"And they overcame him* [the wicked one] *by the blood of the Lamb and by the word of their testimony, and they did not love their lives to the death."*

I believe that in part it means when what's coming out of our mouths (our testimony) agrees with what the blood of Jesus *speaks or decrees,* the power to overcome is released in our lives! Matthew 18:19 (NKJV) tells us about the power of agreement as it says, *"if two of you agree on earth concerning anything that they ask, it will be done for them by My Father in heaven."* This powerful verse gives us a key to a release from Heaven. We need to agree with the Word first and with what the blood of Jesus testifies and decrees. It decrees what Jesus accomplished on the Cross.

We then need to make it our testimony; and by agreeing with it and each other, we will see supernatural results and answers to prayer. We often fail to recite the rest of the verse, however, which is *"they did not love their lives to death."* Someone could make the argument that the qualifier for the first part of the verse—that being us having the power to overcome by the blood of the Lamb and by our testimony—is contingent on dying to self and to the flesh. When we surrender our lives to Christ and He truly becomes Lord over our lives, we die to the dictates and lordship of the flesh and its carnal desires, thereby releasing the overcoming power of the blood of the Lamb.

It's time for the church to reemphasize the blood in our teaching and preaching, in our worship songs, and in our testimonies! To come into agreement with what the blood decrees and see miracles of supernatural intervention as they saw in the book of Acts.

I have felt compelled for some time to write this book, and I greatly appreciate the invitation of the publisher to do so as the church at large needs to be reminded and understand all that the blood of Jesus decrees. As we see it become prevalent in our teaching, preaching, singing, and writing as evangelical Christians, there will once again be great grace and great power in the church that is called by His name.

ONE

The Blood's Decree

What do I mean when I say, "The Blood's Decree"? I've chosen the title *The Blood's Decree* because *a decree* is powerful. So, let's first examine exactly what a decree is.

Merriam-Webster's Dictionary defines the word *decree* as follows:

- an order usually having the force of law, a judicial decree
- a religious ordinance enacted by council or titular head, a papal decree
- a foreordaining will, God's decree
- a judicial decision of the Roman Emperor
- to command or enjoin by or as if by decree
- to determine or order judicially, decree a punishment

As we can see by these definitions, the word *decree* carries a legal aspect to it. A decree definitely evokes a response and cannot be ignored. In fact, there are consequences for not heeding a decree, either positive or negative.

When used in conjunction with the blood of Jesus, decree conveys the powerful truth that the blood of Jesus and His work on the Cross at Calvary provided us as believers the legal right to claim and to lay hold of what He, Jesus, purchased for us with His blood and what His blood speaks over us even today!

The church may not have always comprehended this and thereby may have forfeited much of the blessing, rights, and provisions of Calvary out of ignorance of this powerful truth.

In Bible days when a covenant was made between two individuals or God with an individual, there was usually a sacrifice made, a shedding of blood that sealed the covenant. That blood spoke a testament of all that the covenant entailed—it's power and provisions, terms and conditions. It was binding and could not be broken. The application of the blood by Abraham, Isaac, Jacob, Moses, David, and so on was done with the knowledge and understanding that God was vowing to do what He promised He would do and that His Word is immutable, or unchanging and "forever settled." That He is the God who cannot lie. They could stake their very lives and future on it, knowing His Word is final.

In the United States when someone is in police custody and suspected of committing a crime, the person must be made aware of their legal rights, including their Miranda rights informing them of their fifth and sixth amendment rights that include the right to remain silent and to be represented, that their words may be used, and so forth.

Even to us believers today, we must realize our rights in Christ and that the promises of God are blood-backed and sealed. If He said it, He will do it! His blood decrees so!

When the "accuser of the brethren," a name given in Scripture in Revelation 12:10 to the adversary of our souls, the devil himself, brings charges against us, we must know our scriptural, legal rights as believers that the blood of Jesus speaks over us.

We must declare those rights in agreement with what the blood speaks!

We must speak what the blood says and decree it over our lives to realize the full potential of what Christ's victory has won for us.

One more thing....when I was growing up, our mom would often ask us to do some things she wanted us to do. If we replied "why?" In protest, she would reply "because I said so!" Not being mean or overbearing, just reminding us emphatically of her authority as our mom! Well, I'd like to take the phrase "because I said so" and employ it for us to use when stating what the blood decrees over us. "The blood says so!" When I preach this message, I will often state one of the "better things" that the blood speaks, decrees, and have them respond with "because the blood says so!" I encourage you to do the same as you are reading this book and claim what your inheritance is, spoken by the blood of Jesus!

TWO

Jesus' Signet Ring

The Lord Jesus engraved His image on us with His signet ring, His precious blood that decrees.

A signet ring was worn by the head of a household, a high government official, a king, or a governor, as was the case with Zerubbabel, a governor in Israel after the people returned from captivity in Babylon.

A signet ring's emblem was unmistakably the official insignia of that particular governor, king, or official. Any official decree or document from the official would be sealed with wax and stamped with the emblem on the signet ring. This afforded the recipient the knowledge that this was the official word and had to be not only received but enacted. It spoke in no uncertain terms to "Take this message seriously! Pay attention to it and heed its mandates!" The signet ring's stamp was the voice, if you will, of the official speaking or decreeing.

As mentioned, Zerubbabel was the governor of the rebuilt Jerusalem and was himself of royal blood, being a descendant of David and the grandson of Judah's King Jehoiachin. It had been prophesied by the prophet Haggai and is written for us in the book that bears his name that Zerubbabel is called *"my signet ring."*

In Haggai 2:23 (NIV) we read, *"'On that day,' declares the Lord Almighty, 'I will take you, my servant Zerubbabel son of Shealtiel,' declares the Lord, 'and I will make you like my signet ring, for I have chosen you.'"* What did God mean when He said Zerubbabel was His signet ring?

Years earlier, Jehoiachin had lost his throne when he was deported to Babylon; in fact, God pictured Jehoiachin as a signet ring being removed from God's finger (Jeremiah 22:24). Now, God calls Zerubbabel the "signet ring," but this time it wouldn't be removed.

In the prophecy of Haggai, God is giving Zerubbabel hope and divine encouragement, assuring him that he was chosen for this time and unique assignment. Also, in so doing, God was reinstating the Davidic line and renewing the covenant He made with David. Judah still had a future to look forward to—the coming of the "Son of David," the Messiah who would one day overturn thrones and obliterate the power of earthly kingdoms.

Sealed and Irrevocable

In the famous story in the book of Esther, we find another example of the signet ring's use. God brought about deliverance for the Jews by raising up Esther, a prophetess. There's a powerful example of the authority, weight, and irrevocability of what a king's signet was and is!

Esther 8:8 (NKJV) says, *"You yourselves write a decree concerning the Jews, as you please, in the king's name, and seal it with the king's signet ring; for whatever is written in the king's name and sealed with the king's signet ring no one can revoke."*

Relating that to our spiritual inheritance spoken by the blood of Jesus, whatever is written in the King Jesus's name and sealed (by the blood) with the King's signet ring, no one can revoke.

Hallelujah! Whatever the blood of our King Jesus decrees is irrevocable!

THE PRODIGAL SON

A New Testament example of the power of the signet ring is seen in the familiar story of the Prodigal Son found in Luke's Gospel, chapter 15. Most are familiar with the phrase "prodigal son." Even if they are not practicing Christians, they know of it through literature and dramatic presentations down through history.

As the story goes, a wealthy, powerful man had two sons and one day the younger came to the father and asked him to give him his inheritance. The father granted his request and gave him the portion of his fortune that would be his. A few days later he was off to a far country where he wasted all of his inheritance. In his rebellion and lack of appreciation for what he had at his father's house, the son took the money and squandered it on riotous living, irresponsibly frittering away it all.

In time, the son finds himself destitute and impoverished to the point that he winds up eating the food the pigs ate. The opposite of a "rags to riches" story, he went from riches to ruin. At a point of desperation and hunger, it finally dawns on the son that he had it pretty good in his father's house and that there was an abundance of food there to satisfy his hunger, so he decides to make his way home.

When the father sees him, yet still a far off, he came running with compassion to welcome him back. Undeservedly, yet in character of a true father, the father receives him without regard for the son's previous disrespect.

Not only does the father welcome him home but calls for his servants to bring his best robe and puts it on his son; he then puts a ring on the son's finger and also shoes on his feet. Each of these gifts is powerfully significant, especially the ring.

The robe is a picture of the robe of righteousness we receive by the blood of Jesus when we come to Him from having been in another country, spiritually separated from our Father's house. Just as the young son, we are totally underserving of it but it is put on us or imparted to us because of the mercy of the Father.

The ring that the father put on his child's finger was not just any ring, it was the father's *signet ring!* This ring represented the father, his authority, and was a symbol of his stature, which was also used to seal documents transacted by him. The son was given back the authority of all that ring stood for in that moment. It voiced the father's heart and will for his son—just as the blood of Jesus speaks the Father's heart and will for us. As the prodigal son in this story, we are unworthy to possess it, yet it is offered by our heavenly Father without hesitation.

Only sons wore sandals, not the servants of the household. When the father put sandals on his feet, despite the son saying he was unworthy to be considered a son and would be happy just to be a servant, the father was saying your sonship is restored, your place in the family is unquestioned. Such an amazing picture of what happens when a soul comes to Christ and receives salvation through the blood of Jesus!

Amazing Grace

All of this the blood decrees over us, and we need often to remind ourselves of such amazing grace spoken by the blood.

What an amazing picture of the grace of our heavenly Father and the love of Jesus, our Savior! Christ has put His robe of righteousness and His signet ring on us, raising us up to be joint heirs with Him to share in His authority—just as the act of the father putting sandals on the son's feet declared he was a son.

The blood's decree is stamped and sealed by the signet ring of the Lord Himself. As was the case in both these Old Testament and New Testament examples of how powerful the signet ring was, let's recall the last phrase of Esther 8:8 (NKJV) that declares *"whatever is written in the king's name and sealed with the king's signet ring no one can revoke."* The stamp of the blood of Jesus, our King, the King of kings is irrevocable! It cannot be challenged or reversed because Jesus' blood decrees it so. We can trust it!

In the prophetic sense, you and I have been stamped with the mark or emblem of our King Jesus and we carry the official word and authority of the King in us, thus we are also His signet ring. We, too, have been chosen for this time and our specific assignment to decree the Word of the Lord. We need to understand that we also are included in the covenant—the covenant of Jesus' blood *"...that speaks better things than that of Abel"* according to Hebrews 12:24 (NKJV).

The stamp on our hearts is the blood of Jesus, the blood that speaks! This prophecy was not only for the time of Christ on earth, but also a millennial prophecy, prophecy of the thousand-year reign of the Lord.

We carry the authority of His office with us and in us by the blood and so when we speak according to what it speaks, it gets the attention of the spirit world. Just as was the case with the Old Testament kings, the Word of the King of kings, Jesus Christ's Word, is irrevocable and carries the authority of His office as Prophet, Priest, and King. What an amazing thought that we are joint heirs with Christ and in like manner carry that authority as well! Time for the church—those who have been sealed by the

King's signet ring, the blood that decrees—to make an imprint on our generation, our society for the Kingdom of Christ!

Do you realize that you and I are kings and priests today? Revelation 1:6 (NKJV) says, *"And has made us kings and priests to His God and Father; to Him be glory and dominion forever and ever. Amen."* The blood of Jesus has made us kings and priests. Therefore, when we speak, we speak as that of kings and priests.

Look what God's Word says about the word of kings and priests. Ecclesiastes 8:4 (NKJV) says, *"Where the word of a king is, there is power."* Deuteronomy 21:5 states in paraphrase, that priests have the authority to declare things *"settled"* and it will be as they say. Our words carry weight in the spiritual world. Our words are powerful as kings and priests under the King of kings and our High Priest, Jesus Christ. We bear His signet and have the authority to decree things settled as priests.

His Authority Is Our Authority

I won't go into detail about this but about 15 years ago my wife and were facing an extremely difficult problem and conflict. No matter how we prayed, it just wouldn't seem to budge, and it went on and on causing distress. One day, in prayer, we took hold of this truth in Scripture and the Holy Spirit quickened to our understanding that as a king and as priest, we had the authority to speak and declare it settled with the backing of the King's blood, His Word. We did so and before God, I can tell you that within a short time that situation began to turn around. The devil is put on notice when we voice the authority of our King! His Word, His decree set things in motion in the heavenly realm.

Is it any wonder that when Jesus was giving instruction to the disciples on how to pray in Matthew chapter 6, He said to pray that it would be *"on earth as it is in heaven"?* He was telling us to pray that our reality on earth would be as it is in Heaven. Well then, how is it in Heaven? Is there sickness or disease there? The answer of course is an emphatic, "No!" Is there poverty or lack there? Again, "No!" Is there oppression or mental torment there? "No!" You get the idea! We have the powerful vehicle of prayer to voice the will of the King and believe that His blood has spoken into our impossible situations, causing miraculous interventions—and when necessary, angelic assistance in our time of need.

Back to Zerubbabel for a moment. You may likely remember that Zerubbabel is the one the prophet Zechariah addresses and prophesies over in the well-known passage of Scripture in Zechariah 4. Zerubbabel was trying to rebuild the walls of the temple that had been destroyed, and he was facing opposition while attempting to do so. The prophet characterizes the opposition and challenge Zerubbabel is facing as a mountain, and says, *"Who are you, O great mountain? Before Zerubbabel you shall become a plain!"* (Zechariah 4:7 NKJV). He prophesies that it will become a plain, a flat land, allowing passage and so forth. In the verse before, the prophet utters the famous words, *"This is the word of the Lord to Zerubbabel: 'Not by might nor by power, but by My Spirit,' says the Lord of hosts"* (Zechariah 4:6 NKJV).

Also in Zechariah 4:7, the prophet Zechariah says, *"And he* [Zerubbabel] *shall bring forth the capstone* [prophetic of Christ Jesus, I might add] *with shouts of 'Grace, grace to it!'"* The Holy Spirit is the Spirit of Grace. They were saying the breath of the Spirit of God to accomplish His will. We need to understand that the Spirit of God enables us to speak what the blood decrees and when we do, we can expect the Spirit of the Lord, the Holy Spirit to perform miracles, remove the obstacles blocking the work of the Lord in Jesus' name.

In the wake of the "woke" philosophy that has permeated society, culture, and sadly governments and even the church in some cases, it's time for us, the blood-washed, to speak up, to voice the Word of the King and push back against the tide of evil! We have all the backing of the King! We have all of His weapons of warfare at our disposal! Time to employ them! Time to decree what the blood says is rightfully ours! Time to declare His Truth unabashedly without fear of reprisal. To *be* the church, not just *attend* church. As the apostle Paul says in Galatians 5:1 (NKJV), to *"Stand fast therefore in the liberty by which Christ has made us free and be not entangled again with a yoke of bondage."* The imagery portrayed here would be that of a line of soldiers holding the line with locked arms and advancing forward toward the enemy.

We are called to understand that we have been stamped with the blood of Jesus, His signet, and because we are now recipients of all the *better things* that His blood decrees, we need to be used as His signet ring.

Hebrews 12:24 states that the blood of Jesus speaks! So then, what are the *better things* that the blood of Jesus speaks? Throughout the remainder of this book, I innumerate the many awesome things that the blood decrees for us as believers.

THREE

THE BLOOD STILL SPEAKS! IT STILL DECREES!

Hebrews 12:24 (NKJV) says, *"To Jesus the Mediator of the new covenant, and to the blood of sprinkling that* ***speaks*** *better things than that of Abel."*

Most in the body of Christ understand that when Jesus shed His blood on Calvary for us, it *decreed* or *spoke* salvation, redemption, healing, deliverance, grace, and much more. When Jesus uttered those final words, *"It is finished,"* or as it is interpreted into Greek, *tetelestai,* His voice resounded through the universe declaring that the battle was over, that He had won the victory over death, hell, and the grave! That with His blood, He bridged the gap between the Holy God and a fallen creation, stained with sin. The wrath of God was satisfied—His wrath against the evil one who deceived and ensnared humankind through the fall of Adam and Eve in the Garden—and the penalty, the price, was paid forever making a way to the throne of God through His precious blood.

What we may not have realized—and to be honest with you, it wasn't until some years back that this truth was made *rhema* or alive to me—is that the blood of Jesus *still* speaks! The blood of Jesus *still* decrees! This revelation, quite frankly, hit me like a ton of bricks.

The blood speaking wasn't a one-time occurrence but rather, according to Hebrew 12:24, it *speaks, now!* It decrees, present tense, right now even more than 2,000 years later!

Even a cursory read of Genesis makes clear that *Jesus spoke* the worlds, the creation into being. His very words have creative power! No wonder Proverbs 4:22 tells us that His law or His Word is life and health to our whole body. And Colossians 1:17 (NKJV) tells us *"And He is before all things, and in Him, all things consist."* He not only set the world in motion with His spoken word, but it is His very word that is holding things together now. His word is still causing this earth and the planets to revolve around the sun and is the very cause for everything in them to consist.

In the same manner, His precious blood is still speaking life, health, power, strength, and so much more! I pray the truth contained in that verse will impact you as it has me, settle deep in your spirit, and cause you to live in the reality of what this truth from the Word of God, the Bible, affords us on a daily basis.

The blood decreeing or speaking was clearly foreshadowed in that God would speak to Israel from the mercy seat in the tabernacle in the wilderness. Keep in mind that this was where the glory of God, *Kabod* in Hebrew, dwelt. Exodus 25:22 tells us that it was from between the two cherubim on the mercy seat that *the Lord would speak to Israel*, further substantiating and prophetically speaking of Hebrews 12:24, which states that *"the blood of sprinkling that speaks"* (Hebrews 12:24 NKJV).

> And there I will meet with you, ***and I will speak with you from above the mercy seat,*** from between the two cherubim which are on the ark of the Testimony, about

> everything which I will give you in commandment to the children of Israel (Exodus 25:22 NKJV).

The mercy seat was a prophetic of the Messiah, Jesus our Savior, and the blood that was applied to it was a symbol of the blood of Jesus. Again, in Exodus 25:22 the Lord says, *"There I will meet with you* [or commune with you], *and I will speak with you…."*

When we today testify of the blood and decree what the blood decrees, the glory of God is present also.

Here we see a clear picture of the blood of Jesus speaking, decreeing centuries before He shed His blood on Calvary. That blood on the mercy seat spoke prophetically of the finished work of Jesus on Calvary and the *better things* that His sacrifice has provided for us today! The Word of God is so amazing, isn't it?! Jesus is our *Ark of Testimony* as cited in Exodus 25:22—His blood speaks (testifies) His victory over mankind's rebellion of God's laws.

SCIENCE, BLOOD, AND THE MEDIATOR

Over the past number of decades, amazing discoveries in technology have made it possible for medical science to now determine various diseases in the body. In a sense, *the blood speaks* signaling whether there may be a malady or cancer developing that could jeopardize the health of the individual. The blood of the individual "speaks," telling doctors what may be wrong in the body. Even forensic science has progressed to the degree that by examining the blood of the deceased or the blood left behind by the perpetrator(s) of the crime, the tale of what happened is told and the criminal identified without the person physically being there.

The blood of Jesus—who is not deceased but alive and sits at the right hand of the Father in Heaven—speaks and declares powerful things for those of us who follow Him, even though we have never seen Him.

So now, Hebrews 12:24 declares the blood of Jesus, the Mediator of the New Covenant speaks! Again, Hebrews 12:24 says, *"And to Jesus the Mediator of the new covenant, and to the blood of sprinkling, that speaks better things than that of Abel."*

The Merriam-Webster dictionary defines *mediator* as: "one that mediates, *especially* one that mediates between parties at variance." An example of mediator used in a sentence: If you two cannot resolve this argument on your own, we'll have to bring in a *mediator.*

Jesus, our Lord and Savior, became just that for you and me, our Mediator, between two parties at variance—a holy, righteous God and sinful humankind.

How did He mediate between us? By sprinkling His precious blood *that speaks!* His blood *that decrees!*

Let's again look closely at Hebrews 12:24 (NKJV) that says, *"To Jesus the Mediator of the new covenant, and to the blood of sprinkling that speaks better things than that of Abel."* Did you catch that? It doesn't say that the blood spoke, or has spoken, it says *"that speaks"!* Present tense! I have looked up the word *speaks* in the original Greek and I can assure you it means just that. Now! Presently! The blood of Jesus is speaking. What an awesome truth this is!

In fact, one of the definitions of the word in Greek for *speaks* is "preaches." I love that! The blood not only speaks, but it's also *preaching* to us daily. I've heard a lot of great preachers in my day, but I've never heard a better Preacher than the blood of Jesus that preaches *better things* for the believer in Christ Jesus!

Directly after that the verse says, *"that speaks* ***better things*** *than that of Abel."* Abel's blood cried out from the grave for vengeance after his brother, Cain, slew him out of a jealous rage. Cain's offering was rejected because it did not contain a blood sacrifice as Abel's did. The importance being that the prophetic significance of the blood Jesus needed to be represented, foreshadowing the work of the Redeemer on the Cross. The writer is saying that what Jesus' blood decrees is so much better than what Abel's does.

Jesus' blood speaks *better things!* Well, if you're like me, you want to know exactly what are the *"better things"* that the blood speaks?! In the following chapters, I present the many powerful better things that the blood of Jesus *speaks, decrees, and preaches* to us, and how knowing this can take our faith and walk with Christ to even deeper levels.

FOUR

The Blood Decrees Redemption

As humans, we love redemption stories. Our movies, literature, and folklore focus heavily on someone trying to make up for a mistake or tragedy in their past. Movies that focus on an underdog or someone who came back from a drastic setback in life or overcame despite extreme obstacles, grab our attention and pull us in.

In many ways, the Bible is a story of redemption. On a macro level, it's the story of humanity's fall, our broken relationship with our Creator, and then God's plan for reconciliation and redemption. Throughout the narrative, we see how God is constantly in the redemption business. The blood of Jesus decrees or tells the greatest redemption story of all! The love of God for fallen man and His eternal plan to redeem us from the hands of the devil.

The Bible doesn't simply tell the tale of humanity's redemption in the abstract, it also gives us individual tales of redemption. Abraham, Moses, and David all committed sin and we are witnesses to their repentance and redemption. For redemption to work in the grand scheme of God's perfect plan, it needs to operate on an individual basis, too.

Throughout the Old Testament there are many types and shadows of the work of Jesus on the Cross that would purchase our redemption.

In the book of Genesis, this foreshadowing is seen in the fact that after Adam and Eve sinned, they realized they were naked and needed a covering. Before that, the glory of God clothed them. In order for the coverings to be made, animals had to be killed and blood had to be shed as Genesis 3:21 (KJV) tells us: *"Unto Adam also and to his wife did the Lord God make coats of skins, and clothed them."* It's a clear prophetic picture of Calvary and the blood that covers us as believers.

As mentioned earlier, redemption is also seen in the well-known story of Noah's ark in that when the waters subsided after many days, the ark rested on the 17th day of the 7th month of the Hebrew calendar. Are you aware that Jesus, our precious Lord and Savior, was crucified on the 14th of the 7th month of the Hebrew calendar and that He rose three days later on the 17th day of the Hebrew calendar? That ark, which Moses obediently built, was a prophetic picture of Jesus, our "Heavenly Ark," our Redeemer and Savior. He became our Heavenly Ark who carried us to safety spiritually; the curse was broken and a way was made for redemption!

In fact, the place where the ark rested was on Mount Ararat. *Ararat* means "the curse is reversed"! When Noah and his family stepped out of the ark, they were walking on curse-free ground. Today, because of Jesus, who decrees redemption, we have been lifted by our Heavenly Ark, Christ Jesus, to also walk on curse-free ground! The curse is broken, and we have been made free by the blood of Jesus! The blood decrees we walk on curse-free ground. The blood decrees we've been saved; we've been redeemed.

I don't know about you, but this truth makes me want to shout, "Hallelujah!"

Another clear picture of redemption is seen in the tabernacle in the wilderness, which the book of Exodus describes in detail. The first entrance, or what was called The Gate, was made of up four colors:

1. *Purple,* representing royalty as seen in Matthew's Gospel, Jesus the King;
2. *White,* representing perfection as seen in Mark's Gospel, Jesus the Perfect Man;
3. *Scarlet,* representing Jesus the suffering Savior as seen in Luke's Gospel, Jesus the Savior;
4. *Blue,* representing Jesus as the Son of God, as seen in John's Gospel.

As King (purple) I obey Him; as the Perfect Man (white) I identify with Him; as Savior (scarlet) I surrender to Him; and as the Son of God (blue) I worship Him.

Let's walk through the tabernacle in the wilderness together. Once through The Gate, we see the brazen altar where sacrifices were made on behalf of Israel's sins. It spoke prophetically of our being justified by the blood of Jesus, which speaks redemption for us today.

Then we come to the laver, a basin made of mirrors where the priest would wash his hands and feet. It represents Jesus, the Word of God, by which we are sanctified according to John 17:17 (NKJV), *"Sanctify them by Your truth. Your word is truth."* Then the priest would pass from the outer court through the five pillars into the Holy Place. Those five pillars represent the five offices of the church: apostle, prophet, evangelist, pastor, and teacher. Amazing, right?!

Once through the pillars, to the right, facing south was the lampstand representing Jesus, the light of the world. To the left, facing north, was the table of shewbread with 12 loaves of bread on it representing the 12 tribes of Israel—and Jesus, the Bread of Heaven.

Next we come to the altar of incense that represents Jesus, our Intercessor, as the Scripture tells us that He always lives to make intercession for us. As Hebrews 7:25 (NKJV) says, *"Therefore He is also able to save to the uttermost those who come to God through Him, since He always lives to make intercession for them."*

In order to go into the most holiest chamber of all called the Holy of Holies, we need to pass through a veil to see the final piece of furniture, the Ark of the Covenant. The box is overlaid with gold with a solid slab of gold as the lid—the mercy seat covering it. It was here that the high priest put the blood of the sacrifice, which spoke of redemption. Every facet of the tabernacle speaks of Jesus, His office, and His work.

I have only touched on the many symbolisms that are contained in the tabernacle. An extensive study will reveal so many more clear revelations of Jesus.

It is interesting to note that the religious Pharisees of Jesus' day became enraged when He says that He is "the Way, the Truth, and the Life." Why? The three entrances of the tabernacle were called "The Way, The Truth, and The Life," so He was proclaiming Himself to be the prophetic fulfillment of the tabernacle and greater than one of the most sacred things in their Jewish religion. If you've not had the opportunity to study the tabernacle, do make time; you will be so blessed and will receive such revelation of redemption!

In fact, if you were to have taken an aerial view of the tabernacle, you would have observed that the placement of the furnishings—the brazen altar, laver, candlestick, table of shewbread, altar of incense, and the Ark of the Covenant—form a cross. I do not believe this is just a coincidence! How amazing that God would foreshadow the instrument of our redemption, the Cross on which Jesus' blood would be poured out, the blood that decrees, in the very design and structure of the tabernacle!

Arguably, the most often quoted and well-known passage of Scripture about redemption is Isaiah 53:4-5 (NKJV):

> Surely He has borne our griefs and carried our sorrows; yet we esteemed Him stricken, smitten by God, and afflicted. But He was wounded for our transgressions, He was bruised for our iniquities; the chastisement of our peace was upon Him, and with His stripes we are healed.

The Hebrew word for *peace* in verse 5 is the word *shalom,* meaning "completeness, soundness, welfare, health, prosperity, and tranquility." Some definitions define *peace* as "total well-being: for body, mind, soul and spirit." You will hear "shalom" spoken often in the Holy Land when someone is saying farewell or good-bye. The word is actually a blessing. When you say "shalom," you are asking for God's blessing of all these definitions on the person.

We as born-again believers understand that peace or shalom is the fruit of the Lord's Spirit present inside our hearts. No true Christian is ever without His peace that passes all understanding.

Philippians 4:7 (NKJV) says, *"And the peace of God, which surpasses all understanding, will guard your hearts and minds through Christ Jesus."* Part of our inheritance in Christ Jesus that the blood speaks is His peace. Even Isaiah prophesied it long before the Messiah was born in verses such as: *"For unto us a Child is born, unto us a Son is given; and the government will be upon His shoulder. And His name will be called Wonderful, Counselor, Mighty God, Everlasting Father, Prince of Peace"* (Isaiah 9:6 NKJV).

Isaiah also declared that if we keep our minds on Him, He will keep us in perfect peace. *"You will keep him in perfect peace, whose mind is stayed on You, because he trusts in You"* (Isaiah 26:3 NKJV).

When we accept the Lord Jesus Christ as our Savior and welcome His Holy Spirit into our lives, we become inheritors of this peace—it's part of what Jesus purchased when He redeemed us.

We not only have the peace *of* God, but more importantly, we have peace *with* God. Our standing with the Lord is redeemed and made righteous by His blood. We no longer must live in fear of judgment because the penalty, as Isaiah 53:5 says, has been paid for and we have been bought with a price, the blood of Jesus.

In fact, the word *redeemed* means "to buy back." Our souls were indeed purchased by the blood of Jesus and we have been bought back from the slavery of sin.

His blood is the currency used in the transaction. It says, "you are Mine!" Satan no longer has possession of us! He has no right, no claim—because the blood says so! No greater price could He have paid than to lay down His life for us, shedding His precious blood. The old song says, "He paid a debt He did not owe; I owed a debt I could not pay...." No possession that this world has to offer is worth more than our redemption!

Some other salient verses in the Bible that speak of our redemption:

> Isaiah 44:22 (NKJV): *"I have blotted out, like a thick cloud, your transgressions, and like a cloud, your sins. Return to Me, for I have redeemed you."*
>
> Colossians 1:14 (NKJV): *"In whom we have redemption through His blood, the forgiveness of our sins."*
>
> Titus 2:14 (NKJV): *"who gave Himself for us, that He might redeem us from every lawless deed and purify for Himself His own people, zealous for good works."*

In the custom and tradition of the day, if a man died prematurely, leaving a wife and perhaps children, a family member, a near kinsman would redeem her and the children, making them his own family. A beautiful example of this is in the story of Ruth in the Bible.

Ephesians 1:7 (NKJV) says, *"In Him we have redemption through His blood, the forgiveness of sins, according to the riches of His grace."* There's no doubt that one of the *better things* (and most assuredly, *the* best thing) that the blood of Jesus decrees is redemption!

The Bible declares in Psalm 107:2 (NKJV), *"Let the redeemed of the Lord say so, whom He has redeemed from the hand of the enemy."* When the true redemptive work of Jesus has transformed you from death to life, from darkness to light, from the bondage of sin to the glorious liberty we have in Christ, you indeed want to say so! You want to speak what the blood speaks!

DECREE

Say this now with me: "I have been redeemed by the blood of the Lamb; Jesus purchased my salvation with His precious blood. I now walk in newness of life; old things having passed away and all things have become new. I am not my own; I belong to Jesus and He has placed His Holy Spirit in me. The blood says so!"

Let's examine another glorious *better thing* that the blood decrees—righteousness.

FIVE

The Blood Decrees Righteousness

Because God is righteous, every act of God is marked by complete righteousness. Likewise, God's people should be marked by their righteousness. However, because all people fall short of the righteousness required to have salvation, no one can be part of God's people if it were not for the righteousness of Jesus Christ who not only died to take our sins but now stands in our place as our righteousness (Romans 3:23; 1 Corinthians 1:30). The righteousness required for salvation is now through faith, and those who have faith in Jesus are marked by practicing righteousness.

The Scripture tells us about our father in the faith, Abraham, who believed God and it was accounted or credited to him for righteousness. Genesis 15:6 (NIV) says, *"Abram believed the Lord, and he credited it to him as righteousness."* This verse is also referenced in the New Testament in Romans 4:3, Galatians 3:6, and James 2:23.

By believing the Word of God, Abraham was credited as righteous. Scripture makes it clear in Galatians 3:7 (NIV) that *"that those who have faith* [faith in Christ Jesus] *are children of Abraham."* In like manner, when we believe in the Lord Jesus Christ and what His blood accomplished for us and speaks over us, we too are credited with righteousness. This righteousness has nothing to do with our own merits; it is imparted to us by the Spirit of the Lord because of *His* righteousness. There's nothing we can do to earn it! There's nothing we can do to be worthy of it! It is transferred to us by believing in the Lord Jesus Christ.

Second Corinthians 5:21 (NKJV) states, *"For He made Him who knew no sin to be sin for us, that we might become the righteousness of God in Him."* Jesus was sinless! Yet, in His mercy and compassion for us, for our sake, He took on sin and the penalty or punishment in our stead so that we could once again stand righteous before the holy God.

Once you are a born-again believer in Christ Jesus, your standing with Him and before God the Father is righteous! It is a work of His grace in us. I am very much aware that some interpret the grace of the Lord and 2 Corinthians 5:21 almost as a license to sin and live an immoral lifestyle. When questioned about this mindset, they say in defense, "I'm the righteousness of God in Him."

Yes, our standing before the Lord is righteous. It's not about our behavior or our works, that is true. However, we mustn't trample God's grace toward us and expect that despite us doing whatever the flesh lures us into doing, there will be no consequences. If we desire to maintain intimacy with Christ and fellowship of His Spirit, we will choose to walk in righteousness and godly living.

Sin Versus Temptation

Once the Spirit of the Lord transforms us into a new creation in Christ, old things pass away. Old things like the desire to sin willfully and without regard for the law of God. At salvation,

He writes His law on our hearts and now our desire is to walk in purity and righteousness before Him. There's a difference between willful sin and yielding to a temptation and thereby sinning. The regenerated heart, the heart that is washed in the blood of Jesus, no longer desires the things that our former carnal nature longed for.

Should we fall into sin however, as we all do from time to time, the Scripture is clear that *"if we confess our sins, He is faithful and just to forgive us our sins and to cleanse us from all unrighteousness"* (1 John 1:9 NKJV). That forgiveness and that cleansing is by the blood of Jesus. The blood speaks forgiveness, cleansing, and the righteousness of God in Christ.

The prophet Isaiah spoke prophetically of what happens when we come to Jesus at salvation in Isaiah 1:18 (NKJV), *"'Come now, let us reason together,' says the Lord: 'Though your sins be as scarlet, they shall be as white as snow; though they are red like crimson, they shall be as wool.'"* When we gaze out our window at the freshly fallen snow, we catch a glimpse of its purity. When the Father looks at us, in similar fashion, He sees the purity of the Son.

JUSTIFICATION

At salvation we receive *justification,* that is freedom from the *penalty* of sin because Jesus took the punishment for us on the Cross as Isaiah 53:5 (NKJV) declares: *"He was wounded for our transgressions* [sins], *He was bruised for our iniquities* [generational tendency toward sin]; *the chastisement* [punishment or penalty] *for our peace was upon Him, and by His stripes we are healed."* The Sunday School saying I was taught was that *justified* means "*just as if* we never sinned."

To live a righteous life *after* we are saved, we must experience *sanctification*—or the power of God working in us to overcome temptation and sin's hold on us. Sanctification comes by the Word of God. Sanctification frees us from the *power* of sin over us.

The apostle John writes in the book that bears his name: *"Sanctify them by Your truth. Your word is truth"* (John 17:17 NKJV).

"Sanctified by the word" is a phrase from the Bible that refers to being set apart from the world and made obedient to God's Word. The Greek verb *hagiazo* is used to describe this process. *Hagiazo* means "to make holy, to purify or consecrate. To separate from profane things and dedicate to God" (Strong's 37).

The Holy Spirit makes the Word of God in us powerful to subdue the dictates of the flesh and gives us power over it. In the evil times we are living in, with the emergence of the internet which barrages us 24/7 with the filth of this world, the ungodly mindset of the anti-God culture, as well as the media pumping their corruption right into our homes, it has become more and more difficult to stay pure, to walk in righteousness and live a life separated from the darkness all around us. Only by immersing ourselves in the Word of God and letting it continually sanctify us, giving us power over sin, can we expect to realize the power that the blood of Jesus decrees over us. That blood decrees righteousness!

When I was a young Bible college student, I sang in a trio with my twin brother (who is now with the Lord) and a girl who was in our class at the time. One of the songs we sang was about the blood of Jesus. One of the phrases in the song is, "I've got the blood on the door of my heart...and so when God looks at me, He no more sees the things I've done; He only sees the blood of His crucified Son." The blood on the door of our hearts, speaks the righteousness of Christ. When God looks at us, He sees us through the blood—that blood says *righteous.*

Washing of Regeneration

I love the verse in Titus 3:5 (NKJV) that talks about what happens when we are imparted the righteousness of God at salvation: *"Not by works of righteousness which we have done, but according to His mercy He saved us, through the washing of regeneration and renewing of the Holy Spirit."* If you look at the tense of the word *righteousness* in the original language, it implies a continual washing by the blood of Jesus, not just a one-time occurrence at salvation. What a blessed thought that is; Jesus' blood continually washes us and it regenerates us by the power of the Holy Spirit. Just as the breath of God that breathed into Adam's nostrils caused him to become a living soul and his blood to start circulating, so the breath of the Holy Spirit causes the blood of Jesus, the second Adam, to wash us and regenerate us, making us righteous before God.

Titus 3:5 clearly declares we are not made righteous by any efforts of our own but solely according to the Lord's mercy. Notice it says *"through the washing of regeneration...."* This word *washing,* according to Strong's Concordance is a "bath or baptism." We are baptized into Christ; and as the Holy Spirit washes our hearts, we receive Christ's righteousness.

I think of the well-known story of Jesus' encounter with the Samaritan women at a well in Sychar. Jesus told the disciples that *"He needed to go through Samaria"* (John 4:4 NKJV). It's interesting to note here that Jews generally avoided Samaria because of their bias against the Samaritans. Yet the Master's compassion and love drew Him for a divine encounter with this woman at the well. There, being weary from His journey, He sat down at a well on a parcel of land that Jacob gave to his son Joseph. A woman comes along to draw water and Jesus asks her for a drink.

Keeping in mind the background of the history between Jews and Samaritans, the woman of Samaria says to Him, *"How is it that You, being a Jew, ask a drink from me, a Samaritan woman?"* … *Jesus answered and said to her, "If you knew the gift of God, and who it is who says to you, 'Give Me a drink,' you would have asked Him, and He would have given you living water"* (John 4:9-10 NKJV).

Jesus, the Master Teacher, was using the well to illustrate for her what happens upon salvation that He was offering to her. He goes on to say, *"Everyone who drinks this water will be thirsty again* [meaning the physical well where they were speaking], *but whoever drinks the water I give them will never thirst. Indeed, the water I give them will become in them a spring of water welling up to eternal life"* (John 4:13-14 NIV).

Turns out this woman had quite a sordid past, which Jesus revealed He knew; but in that encounter, when she drank of the living water that He offers, she was made clean, forgiven, righteous and worthy of His presence.

At salvation, a well of water, spiritual life is imparted to us and the water that comes from this well is pure. However, as with natural wells, over time, things can fall into the well and eventually corrupt the water, and in fact, stop the flow all together.

I remember when I was a young boy, my uncle and aunt had a well on their property. On a hot August summer day in New Jersey, my cousins and I would enjoy getting a drink of water from the well. There was a pump handle, and at first we would pump and pump and nothing seemingly was happening. But after a short while, the pump had been primed, and the water would begin to spurt out until it became a continuous stream.

Initially the water that came out of the spout was murky and full of sediment from having been in the pipes for quite a while; nothing we would ever drink! Eventually though, the pure, fresh, cool, revitalizing water began to flow from the well and was a real thirst quencher.

How very much like that is the well of righteousness in Christ Jesus that is in us. Every now and then, we need to allow the Holy Spirit to remove the sediment and dirt that has collected in us by His "washing of regeneration." He will cause our wells to spring up again with living water if we ask Him. I remember singing, "Spring up oh well within my soul, spring up oh well and make me whole; spring up oh well and give to me that life abundantly." Yes, there's a River of Life flowing out of us who know Jesus Christ; and once you've had a taste of that water, nothing that this corrupt world has to offer can compare with it!

Similarly, I'm reminded of the story in Genesis chapter 26:18 where Isaac had to re-dig the wells of his father, Abraham. After Abraham's death, the Philistines, Israel's enemy, had deliberately filled in the wells Abraham had dug. After some digging, those wells began to bring forth water again.

The enemy's tactics haven't changed much over time; he still does everything he can to block our wells spiritually. This may happen through unforgiveness, sinful behavior and acts, prayerlessness, or lack of knowledge of the Word—all of these can block the flow. Thank God we know that the blood of Jesus applied to our hearts can remove every obstacle; all the sediment is gone and replaced with the water of the Lord's righteousness that can flow freely again into our hearts. Speak to your spiritual well in Jesus' name. Tell the waters to spring up! The blood decrees that you are *"the righteousness of God in Him"* (2 Corinthians 5:21 NKJV).

DECREE

Lord, Your Word declares that I am the righteousness of God in Christ Jesus. That if I have believed on You and confessed You with my mouth, I have been saved; I have been washed in the blood and made righteous. It's not about my efforts, my striving or behavior; it's about Your blood that speaks, that decrees I'm righteous today. Cause me to walk in purity before you, separated from anything that pollutes or corrupts, in Jesus' name I pray! Righteousness is mine because...the blood says so!

Praise break! Thank You, Jesus, that Your blood speaks I'm redeemed, I'm made righteous! But wait! There's more!

SIX

The Blood Decrees Reconciliation

Access to the Presence of God

The moment that sin entered the world through Adam and Eve yielding to the temptation of the devil, mankind was separated from God and could no longer walk in fellowship with Him as had previously been their experience. There needed to be a means of *reconciliation* because God is holy and according to His Word cannot even look upon sin. A divine bridge was necessary to span the gap between humankind's disobedience and the Creator. Thankfully, before the foundation of the earth, God in His omniscience (all knowing attribute) planned a way for us to be reconciled to God; otherwise, man would have been eternally separated from Him. This is why Scripture refers to Jesus as *"the Lamb slain from the foundation of the world"* (Revelation 13:8 NKJV).

When Jesus shed His blood on that cruel Cross, just before He gave up His spirit and died, He cried aloud on the Cross, *"It is finished!"* Scripture tells us that the veil of the temple was split in two from top to bottom. Prior to that, only the high priest could go past it into the Holy of Holies and that was only once a year. In fact, a rope with pomegranates and bells was tied to his ankle so that if he touched the Ark of the Covenant and consequently slain, he could be dragged out by that rope.

When the veil (representative of Jesus) was torn in two, it forever spoke access to God! A new and living way was made according to Hebrews, making it possible for the blood-bought people of God to enter the holy presence of God. His blood decreed reconciliation and access to God's throne. His blood spoke no more separation, for a way of access had been made, paid for by the blood of the Lamb.

Today, because the blood decrees so, we, those who have accepted Jesus Christ as Savior and surrendered our hearts to Him, can go boldly to the throne of grace, as Hebrews 4:16 tells us, without fear of reproach or condemnation. We are provided unlimited access to God.

> Let us therefore come boldly to the throne of grace, that we may obtain mercy and find grace to help in the time of need (Hebrews 4:16 NKJV).

What a glorious truth and promise. As blood-washed believers, we have access 24/7, as the expression goes, to the very presence of God, paid for by the blood. We don't have to go through an earthly priest—we have been made worthy by the blood of our High Priest, Jesus, to approach our God and ask for mercy when we have failed or fallen short of His glory—to ask for grace and help in our times of need! The blood's decree is a standing invitation to enter His presence.

I fly quite often and, of course, without a ticket and a boarding pass, I would never be allowed to board a flight. That electronic pass or paper ticket is my assurance that there is a seat for me that has been purchased and to which I have a legal right. Having flown millions of miles with Delta, American, United, and just about every airline you can name because of my frequent flying status, the airlines frequently upgrade me to their comfort seats or even to a first-class seat at times. (No complaints here!) My loyalty to the airlines over the years affords me that privilege.

In Christ Jesus, because of His merits, His grace and mercy, not any of our own, you and I have an entry pass to the presence of God with unlimited benefits that no devil can ever take away from us! Now *that's* an upgrade! Through the blood of Christ we can boldly approach the throne of God and His blood alone. That blood has washed us, and the Holy Spirit imparts grace to us! What a Savior!

Union in Communion

Truth is, at times we feel far from Him and can't seem to sense His presence like we once did. In those times we must trust His Word that promises us He will never leave us or forsake us. Despite what our minds or emotions may be telling us, He is always near. I have found that the blood of Jesus makes us aware of His presence. I love what Ephesians 2:13 (NKJV) says: *"But now in Christ Jesus you who once were far off have been brought near by the blood of Christ."* Of course, this verse is speaking about our redemption, but I believe it can be applied to those times when we don't sense the presence of the Lord also.

When you feel as if God is a million miles away, that your prayers are hitting the ceiling and bouncing back at you, when the circumstances of life have overwhelmed you and you feel completely cut off from the Lord, that's the time to speak what the blood speaks! The Lord is always present when the blood is applied.

I often tell people who are dealing with a particular crisis, whether their health, the health of a loved one, or some situation that seems impossible, to take Communion. There's nothing in Scripture that prevents us from doing so. The Lord makes His presence very real to us when we follow His instruction to *"do this in remembrance of Me"* (Luke 22:19). There's union in the communion!

The blood of Jesus speaks access to His glory and presence and no earthly or demonic force can prevent us from it. The presence of the Lord is with us when the blood is applied. This is clearly seen in the Passover, recorded in the book of Exodus, when the Lord's presence protected the homes from existential threat of the death angel.

The Lord instructed Moses to have the people apply the blood of the sacrifice to the doorposts of their homes, prophetically forming a cross—the instrument where the blood of Jesus would be shed. When the death angel came by, he would be forced to *pass over* their houses because the blood decreed so! Can you imagine the wailing and mourning in the houses of those who were not protected by the blood as their firstborn were killed?! The presence of the blood assured them that they and their loved ones would be spared and shielded from all harm.

When you study the word for *Passover* in Hebrew, you discover that one of the implications of the word *pesach* is that it implies that the Lord *Himself* hovered over the homes of the children of Israel. The clear and awesome truth is that when the blood is applied, the presence of the Lord accompanies it. As revealed earlier, even mentions of the blood and what the blood decrees brings the presence of the Lord into our situations and causes supernatural intervention.

Often, if we are not careful, walls can build up in our relationships that cause estrangement and offenses that seem insurmountable. I know firsthand that the power of the blood can break down the walls and bring reconciliation, not only in our relationship with God but in our earthly relationships as well!

If you are experiencing a similar situation in your family, an estrangement or impasse, and it seems like there's no hope, let me assure you—the blood of Jesus can bring reconciliation and speak peace to the hearts of the individuals involved. It's a trap of the wicked one to make us think there's no hope or there's no remedy. If God could bridge the mighty gulf between sinful humankind and His righteous presence, He can certainly tear down walls of division and separation in our relationships that may have existed for years. Don't settle for the evil one's lie! Plead the blood of Jesus over relationships. Speak the reconciliation that the blood of Jesus speaks and believe God to do it.

Before Jesus gave His life on the Cross, He told the disciples that He would pray for the Father to send *another Comforter* to abide or live with us forever: *"And I will pray the Father, and he shall give you another Comforter, that he may abide with you for ever"* (John 14:16 KJV). The Comforter is the Holy Spirit! The word *comforter* in Greek is the word *paraclete* or "one called alongside to help." If we, the body of Christ, could only realize that we have a Divine Partner, a Divine Helper, who is within us and is always at the ready to help us in our times of need, we would often see supernatural miracles of reconciliation.

Do keep in mind also the words of the apostle Paul: *"we wrestle not against flesh and blood, but against principalities, against powers, against the rulers of the darkness of this world, against spiritual wickedness in high places"* (Ephesians 6:12 KJV). We often make the mistake of thinking that our issue is with a person—whether it's our spouse or friend or whatever the relationship—when actually behind the problem there are principalities and powers and all of what Paul lists here that are at work. Come against them, not the person, in the name of Jesus and decree that the blood of Jesus speaks reconciliation.

We are not in this alone! The Word of the Lord says in Jeremiah 33:3 (NKJV), *"Call to Me, and I will answer you, and show you great and mighty things, which you do not know."* Some have called this verse God's telephone number to call. The Holy Spirit, the Helper, is always near, ready to assist us or to help us in the fight against principalities and powers. The sacrifice of Calvary assures us of it. The blood decrees it!

DECREE

Say this with me: "I have received reconciliation by the blood of the Lamb, and His blood declares that I have unlimited access to the throne of grace! I refuse the lie of the devil that tells me God has forsaken me and that I'm not worthy to be in the presence of my Holy God. The blood has stamped my heart with the blood of Jesus; and when God looks at me, He only sees the blood of His crucified Son. His presence is with me regardless of what may be going on around me. Regardless of what my emotions may be telling me. I agree with the blood that decrees reconciliation and access to the presence of God. I speak the reconciliation of the blood to my relationships and peace in the name of Jesus. The blood decrees it! The blood says so!"

SEVEN

THE BLOOD DECREES HEALING

Since I have spent more than 40 years in healing ministry, this *better thing*, healing, is something I have witnessed over and over; therefore, I have much I'd like to share with you about it! I state unequivocally that there's no way anyone could ever convince me that God doesn't heal today! I do believe you will be blessed by not only the truth in it but by the anecdotal testimonies of healing contained in this chapter as well.

Isaiah prophesied of Jesus, the Healer:

> ***Surely*** He has borne our griefs and carried our sorrows; yet we esteemed Him stricken, smitten by God, and afflicted. But He was wounded for our transgressions, He was bruised for our iniquities; the chastisement for our peace was upon Him, and by His stripes we are healed (Isaiah 53:4-5 NKJV).

The blood decrees healing!

I find it interesting that Isaiah the prophet uses the word *surely* at the beginning of verse 4 when speaking about healing. Notice he doesn't use it at the beginning of the next verse or thought in verse 5, which talks about the work of our redemption.

Could it be that in His omniscience, the Holy Spirit knew that many in our day would have a harder time believing that Jesus still heals as opposed to when Jesus walked the earth and they objected more to Him declaring Himself to be the Son of God sent to be the Savior of the world, the Way, the Truth, and the Life?

Today, it's often the other way around in some of the more mainline churches. Most believers do not have an issue with redemption or salvation by the blood, but when the topic of healing is brought up, many don't believe it's for today. Perhaps that is why a *"Surely"* was necessary to drive home the point that included in the atonement was not only the redemption of our souls but also the healing of our bodies, minds, and emotions.

HEALING AND THE HEALER

That being said, after having witnessed healing in my family and my own life, having spent much time in study of the Word of God, having traveled the world millions of miles to more than 70 countries for healing crusades, having been involved in healing ministry for more than 40 years and seeing thousands of people healed of all kinds of sickness—there is not a shadow of a doubt in my mind that Jesus, the Healer, still heals today! These eyes have seen too much to ever deny it! The blood of Jesus speaks healing!

My mom followed many healing ministries throughout her life as she often needed healing. As a young boy I remember attending a tent crusade in Teaneck, New Jersey, where the well-known healing evangelist Oral Roberts was ministering.

Later we attended a Kathryn Kuhlman service in Pittsburgh, Pennsylvania. Mom had many of the popular books on healing, including the classic by F.F. Bosworth, *Christ the Healer.* I inherited that book and it had a great impact on me. I highly recommend it, particularly if you're in need of healing and especially if you feel called to be used in healing ministry.

I also remember Mom telling me of the account of a miraculous healing testimony that she had read about; a woman by the name of Betty Baxter was healed when she was 15 years old. I've never forgotten the impression it made on me and my faith. I encourage you to do some research and be blessed yourself by this amazing testimony of the healing power of the Lord. Here's what her website says:

> Betty Baxter's miracle is as dramatic as any recorded during the earthly life and ministry of Jesus Christ. Betty suffered progressive spinal scoliosis, paralysis and heart failure. By age fifteen she could not leave her home, confined either to a bed or chair and was too fragile to receive visitors. She was dying. Physicians had nothing to offer in terms of treatment. On August 24, 1941, when she was fifteen years of age, Jesus Christ visited her home and laid His hand on her curved spine. In the presence of multiple eyewitnesses, all of her diseases and musculoskeletal deformities vanished. She leaped from the chair instantly and completely healed.[1]

Many years later, while at an evangelistic healing crusade in Venezuela, this following amazing miracle stands out in my memory. A young mother, who had been brought into the healing service on a stretcher, came for healing. She had been paralyzed

---

1 "Betty Baxter's Miracle"; https://www.bettybaxtermiracle.com/; accessed April 4, 2025.

from the waist down by an epidural shot given to her while she was pregnant and about to deliver her child. Sadly, her husband had left her, not being able to cope with the situation. Her bodily functions were incapacitated, and she had to wear a diaper. She could not even hold her newborn baby. The healing power of the Lord came upon her and she leaped up from that stretcher completely healed! The next day she came to the service dressed beautifully in a red dress with proper shoes holding the baby and giving glory to God for what He had done the night before. We serve a healing Jesus!

The Lord declared to Moses in Exodus 15:26 (NIV), *"I am the Lord, who heals you."* And He still is! He didn't say I *was* the Lord who heals. No. He said, "I *am* the Lord who heals you"!

One of God's attributes is immutableness; He never changes. Hebrews 13:8 (NIV) declares, *"Jesus Christ is the same yesterday and today and forever."* That Scripture clearly declares that Jesus fills the requirement of immutability. Jesus was, is, and will ever be the Lord who heals!

Psalm 107:20 (NKJV) says, *"He sent His word and healed them, and delivered them from their destructions."* John 1:1 (NKJV) tells us, *"In the beginning was the Word* [Jesus], *and the Word was with God and the Word was God."* Jesus is the Word, and the Word was sent to heal and deliver us from our destructions, which includes physical issues. He accomplished His mission on the Cross where He shed His precious blood that decrees, *"with His stripes we were healed"* (Isaiah 53:5 KJV).

We can place our faith in the Word of God, which is truth and which the Bible says is *"Forever... Your word is settled in heaven"* (Psalm 119:89 NKJV) and does not change. Healing is part of the atonement, the work of Jesus Christ on the Cross. With every drop of blood He shed, that blood cried out, *"with His stripes you are healed!"*

Words are powerful! One negative word, or even a word not intentionally meant to harm, can cause our hearts to become fearful, to lose hope and faith, and cause us to spiral down into despair. That's why it is so important that when we speak to others, and to ourselves, that we speak life! Speak and decree in agreement with what the blood speaks over us!

Does that mean we deny reality and pretend that all is well when it's not? No! Some have been erroneously taught that "they can't confess it" referring to a diagnosed illness or malady. But dear reader, I don't see that in the Word of God. The blood is stronger than that! Facts are facts; but the truth of the matter is that what the blood of Jesus decrees can change facts and bring about healing and deliverance.

I'm quite certain that most believers have been to see a doctor a time or two in their life. New patients are required to fill out a checklist of all the diseases that they and their family members have or have had. While I understand that heredity can sometimes play a part in what descendants may deal with physically or otherwise, I do *not* believe that we as believers must accept that those maladies will necessarily come upon us!

As I'm filling out the questionnaire, in my mind I say, *Canceled, canceled...,* as I'm checking off heart disease, diabetes, cancer, and so forth...*by the blood of Jesus!* His blood speaks that the curse is broken! His blood decrees that *"by His stripes we are healed"* (Isaiah 53:5). His blood declares, *"I am the Lord who heals you"* (Exodus 15:26), so I personally would rather agree with what the blood says rather than some expert opinion, as knowledgeable as he or she may be.

Please don't get me wrong here; I am thankful for medical science and for doctors and their knowledge and do believe that we can benefit from them. However, a doctor may tell you a fact—for example, that the tests show the presence of a disease—but I believe the truth of the Word of God that the blood decrees can change facts! In my own family, there has been heart disease, kidney failure, diabetes, and so forth. Let me give you a few personal testimonies of the healing and keeping power of the blood in my own life and my family.

THE POWER OF THE BLOOD

In 2007, my saintly mother—a woman of tremendous faith who had an affinity for healing ministries and been healed many times previously—developed intricate blockages in an area of her heart that were not accessible by traditional angioplasty (the balloon procedure that clears the arteries). She was literally dying in front of us. Her color was ashen and could only walk a few small steps without becoming completely breathless.

At the time, I was living south of Los Angeles, California, and was about to embark on a trip to Berlin, Germany, for ministry. When I boarded the plane, my heart was burdened for my mom, and I prayed fervently for her during the flight. It so "happened" that my connection was in JFK in New York where I had an hour and a half layover before taking the next flight to Berlin. I had switched off my cell phone as one must do during a flight, so after landing in JFK, I turned it on and called my twin brother for an update on Mom's condition. The tone in his voice said it all, followed by the words, "Jim, if you want to see her again in this life, you'd better come because the doctors say she most likely won't make it through the night."

As you can imagine, my heart sank upon hearing those words. Now I was faced with a dilemma; I am supposed to be headed to Berlin, but my mom is dying. I made a few calls and long story short, made the decision to leave the airport, rent a car, and drive two hours to where my mom lived in New Jersey. I got there late at night, hoping and praying I would make it in time. When I walked into the room, I saw my mom's color was gray and she was gasping for breath.

When I whispered, "Mom, it's Jim," she opened her eyes, smiled and said, "Jim, I just want breath to praise Him," meaning Jesus. I immediately responded, "The Lord will give you that breath, Mom." I sat with her for a short time, prayed with her, and tried to be an encouragement but didn't want to wear her out by talking, so I kissed her and started to walk to the door.

Just then the Holy Spirit said to me, "Go get your iPod." Back then we listened to music on an iPod, which preceded having the ability to listen to music on our phones. I went to the car, got my iPod, came back and asked if she'd like to hear the Word of God in her ears as she slept. She said, "Oh yes, that would be wonderful." On my iPod I had a healing Scripture CD with a musical background. Scriptures included Exodus 15:26, *"I am the Lord who heals you";* Isaiah 53:4-5, *"Surely He has borne our sorrows* [sickness in the original] *and carried our sorrows* [pain in the original]...*and by His stripes* [the blood of Jesus that decrees] *we are healed."* All night long the Spirit of the Lord breathed the breath of the Holy Spirit into Mom's being as she heard and meditated on the Word that she loved.

In the morning, anxious to get a report on Mom's condition, I called the hospital and asked for the nurse station on her floor. I asked, "May I have a report on Rachel Cernero?" The nurse said,

"Just a second." A few moments later, I heard my mother's voice, not weak and breathless like a few short hours ago, but strong and loud declare, "Jim, the Lord touched me! I can breathe again! I can praise Him!"

I know without a doubt that the breath of the Spirit quickened her, made her alive by the power of the shed blood of Jesus and His Word! She lived another 10 years until the age of 87 and even sang before an audience of thousands of people at a crusade with her beautiful soprano voice her favorite hymn, "Great Is Thy Faithfulness." To God be the glory. The blood spoke healing to Mom that night!

I remember when my eldest brother passed away 11 years ago at the age of 64 due to kidney disease. The enemy whispered in my ear, "You will probably also die young of kidney disease." For a slight moment, I started to experience pains that led me to believe that he was right. Then, in my spirit, the Word of God rose up and I declared, "You are a liar, satan!" God's Word says, His blood says I am healed and that *none* of these diseases do I have to accept.

The same thing happened five years ago when my beloved twin brother passed away of heart disease. I had to battle against thoughts such as, *Well, you're his twin; you have identical genetics so it's just a matter of time and you'll end up the same way.* Once again, I shouted at him (internally), *That's what you think! The blood of Jesus says, not so!* To this day, I have had no heart issues and have an active life, traveling, ministering, and doing what some men younger than me aren't able to do!

There's power in the blood of Jesus! That power is released when we declare, speak, and decree what it speaks (Hebrews 12:24). I encourage you to do this when you are faced with health challenges and seemingly impossible situations, and I know the Lord will do the same for you as He did and does for me. After all, God shows no favoritism (Acts 10:34 NIV).

When the Lord launched me into a new season of ministry in 2010, after having spent many years in music and worship ministry, the gifts of the Spirit began to flow through me, the word of knowledge, gifts of healing, and so forth. I remember distinctly that I was preaching and ministering at a church in the Dayton, Ohio, area one Sunday morning. As I was preaching, a woman started down the aisle from the back of the auditorium being helped by her daughter. Thinking she would go to a seat and sit down, I kept preaching. But no, she proceeded straight up the pulpit, crying from the pain she was experiencing due to a broken back.

I asked her, "Can I help you?"

She said, "My back, my back is broken and I'm in agony." She was a nurse, and while attempting to lift a large man, her back was broken causing her much pain.

The word of faith rose in me, and I said to her, "Do you believe the Lord can heal right now?"

She said without hesitation, "Yes, yes, I believe!" I asked her where the pain was in her body, and she replied in her lower back. I then asked if she wouldn't mind if I laid my hand on her back to pray for her. She agreed.

When I laid my hand on her back, I felt a brace that wasn't visibly evident because it was hidden under her sweater. Before I could think another thought (which is probably a good thing), I told her, "Take that brace off in faith and the Lord will heal you." To be honest, I didn't know how she was going to be able to do it, but somehow she managed to get it off and the next thing we knew, she screamed, "The pain is gone! There's no more pain!' as the tears streamed down her face. She had been in constant pain for quite a long time and now she was experiencing the healing touch of the Lord. She walked out of that service completely healed, without pain and able to resume her work as a nurse! The blood speaks healing! Glory to His name!

This is just one of many, many examples of those who have been healed by the power of God that I personally have either witnessed or the Lord has used me to be an instrument through which He healed. Blinded eyes have opened, deaf ears have opened, tumors and cysts have disappeared, lameness, arthritis, fibromyalgia, and many more diseases have been healed! The blood decrees healing!

I truly believe that the blood decrees healing for every aspect of our beings, not just for physical healing.

His Shed Blood

This is not original with me, but I love it nonetheless. It's been said that the blood of Jesus was shed seven times. This was prophetically foreshadowed in Leviticus 4:6, which tells us that the priest shall dip his finger in the blood of the sacrifice and sprinkle that blood seven times before the Lord in front of the veil of testimony.

Let's look at each time, noticing how comprehensive the shed blood of Jesus is.

First Time

Jesus was praying in the garden of Gethsemane. Luke 22:44 (KJV) records that His agony was so intense that His sweat was *"as it were great drops as of blood."* While I know there is some differing opinions on whether His sweat became blood or not, some scholars interpret the Scripture to mean those drops appeared to be like blood. I personally believe it was His actual blood. Those drops came from His brow. The brow speaks of the emotions; those drops that fell were for our emotional healing. The blood speaks healing for our emotions.

I am not at all against therapy, it has its use and is helpful to a degree. However, whatever trauma we have may endured emotionally in our past, or presently, can be healed because Jesus paid the price for it to be. Emotional injuries do not have to affect our present or our future; they do not have to become our identity! In Christ, old things are passed away and all things become new. Second Corinthians 5:17 (NKJV) says, *"Therefore, if anyone is in Christ, he is a new creation; old things have passed away; behold, all things have become new." All* things mean *all* things! I believe that includes our emotions.

There's an amazing passage in Isaiah that indicates that the Lord is our rear guard. Isaiah 58:8-9 (NIV) says:

> Then your light will break forth like the dawn, and ***your healing will quickly appear***; then your righteousness will go before you, and the glory of ***the Lord will be your rear guard.*** Then you will call, and ***the Lord will answer***; you will cry for help, and he will say: Here am I.

Did you catch that? Isaiah says the glory of the Lord will be our rear guard! Why would we need a rear guard, you might ask? Aren't most of our battles or troubles ahead of us? I believe these powerful verses tell us prophetically, that because the Lord shed His blood for us, that blood decrees that His glory will block the wounds of the past, the guilt and shame that may have resulted from our sinful actions, the attack of the enemy to use it to thwart or hinder the plans God has to prospers us (Jeremiah 29:11), and liberate us from its hold on us in every way.

The blood speaks protection from even our past! We don't need to stay stuck in the hurt of the past! That was a temporary wound, but it doesn't need to become our identity! In Christ, we have a renewed and restored identity as a victor—not a victim. The blood says so!

Second Time

The second time the blood of Jesus was shed was when He stood before Caiaphas, the high priest. The Bible tells us that Jesus' face was struck and beaten so badly that it was marred beyond recognition as Isaiah the prophet had prophesied it would be. *"Just as there were many who were appalled at him—his appearance was so disfigured beyond that of any human being and his form marred beyond human likeness"* (Isaiah 52:14 NIV).

I believe that Jesus' image was so horribly marred that our image might be transformed into His image. We bear the image of Christ, and our countenance reflects His glory. In fact, we are carriers of His glory because of the brutal beating that Jesus endured on our behalf.

In all humility, people have gasped when I walked into a room. When I gave an inquisitive look as to why the reaction, they have said the glory of God came in the room the moment I walked in. To God be the glory! No greater compliment could ever be given to us than for Jesus Christ to be so evident in us that we usher in His glory and it is reflected on our faces wherever we go. It is all because of the blood of Jesus!

THIRD TIME

The third time the blood was shed was when Jesus stood before Pilate. There they shoved a crown of thorns on His head in mockery of Him, and the blood poured from His skull.

The skull speaks of our minds. Sadly, there is an epidemic of mental illness in our society today. I believe that blood was shed for us to be healed mentally so we can possess a "sound mind" as 2 Timothy 1:7 (NKJV) says we have. I am not ignorant of the fact that some mental issues are physiological in nature resulting from a chemical imbalance. Here again, advances in medical science can be helpful. However, I do believe that even these complexities can be healed by the power of the blood of Jesus. Again, the battlefield of spiritual warfare takes place in the mind. The enemy knows that.

The Greek word *diablolos* means the devil, who strikes over and over at our mind with intrusive, destructive thoughts. Satan is a master at doing just that, striking over and over with his oppressive thoughts. The mature Christian understands that the way to combat evil is to employ the same way Jesus defeated him when tempted in the wilderness after His baptism in water. Each time the devil came to Him and tempted Him, Jesus answered back with an *"It is written!"* declaration. The Bible tells us that afterward the devil left Him.

As mentioned earlier, I had personal experience with this issue as a young Bible college student, which I will share in more detail later in this book, but for now I will tell you most assuredly, it was the Word of God that delivered me. Jesus Christ purchased for us a renewed mind; our minds can be renewed in Him by the power of His Holy Spirit all because of Jesus' work on Calvary when He shed His blood for us.

If you're dealing with recurring thoughts, lustful thoughts, thoughts that are contrary to a renewed and pure mind, and you can't seem to get the victory over them, there is a way out! Declare an *"It is written"* over the wicked one and believe that the blood decrees you have a sound, renewed mind in Christ, and He will bring you out! The blood says so!

Fourth Time

The fourth time Jesus' blood was shed was when they whipped His precious back unmercifully. Historians tells us that the whips used by the Romans had balls that rolled when it struck the back of the individual, tearing out the flesh when extracted. Mel Gibson's depiction in *The Passion of the Christ* movie was extremely graphic; but in truth, I don't believe even that showed the full extent of just how awful that scourging was for our Lord and the agony He endured.

Isaiah prophesied in Isaiah 53:5: *"He was wounded for our transgressions, He was bruised for our iniquities; the chastisement* [punishment] *for our peace was upon Him, and by His stripes we are healed."* With each drop of blood that poured from Jesus' back as He was being beaten, those drops decreed we are healed!

According to Jewish law, a person could only receive 39 lashes, otherwise the person would be degraded to the point of not being human. However, Jesus was scourged under Pilate, or Roman rule. We don't know definitively how many stripes Jesus bore but regardless of the number, it was excruciating and unimaginable torture He endured. If we believe the Bible, the

Word says, *"by His stripes* [regardless the number] *we are healed."* There's no illness that is beyond the scope of the healing power of our Lord Jesus Christ.

As mentioned previously, my eyes have witnessed countless healings of every disease imaginable, and I could never be convinced otherwise of the fact that Jesus heals and that His blood speaks healing for us body, soul, and spirit. Again, I love that Exodus 15:26 (NKJV) says, *"**I am** the Lord who heals you."* The Bible doesn't say I was or I will be—it says, *"I am...!"* Jesus is now our Healer, and we can declare it because...the blood says so!

When I preach this message, I demonstrate the lashes, and with each one I call out a different disease: cancer healed, heart disease healed, and so forth. I have the congregation declare each time, "Because the blood says so!"

There's an account I heard of a man who approached the well-known healing evangelist Oral Roberts in one of his meetings stating, "I don't believe in healing."

In response, it is said that Oral looked at him and then asked him to hand him his Bible. The man did so and then Oral said, "Now give me some scissors."

Puzzled, the man inquired, "Scissors?! Why would you need scissors?"

Oral replied, "You say you don't believe in healing, right? Well, I'm going to cut out every verse in the Bible that talks about Jesus' healing."

The man protested and said, "You can't do that!"

Oral asked him, "Why not?"

The man then said, "That would be destroying my Bible!"

Oral wisely responded, "That's exactly what you do when you say that Jesus doesn't heal; you destroy the Word of God!"

Hebrews 13:8 (NKJV) says, *"Jesus Christ is the same yesterday, today, and forever."* Because He was the Healer back when He walked earth, He's the Healer today! His precious blood decrees through the centuries that by His stripes we are healed, and we can put our complete faith and trust in what His stripes speak!

One more thing to consider about the well-known passage of Scripture in Isaiah 53:4. The prophet prophetically declared, *"Surely He has borne our griefs and carried our sorrows; yet we esteemed Him stricken, smitten of God, and afflicted."* The following verse ends with the words *"and by His stripes we are healed."*

I particularly enjoy looking up words in the Bible in the original language because often there is a depth of meaning and a clearer understanding of the import of the word when doing so. That is the case here in the Isaiah 53:4.

The words *griefs* here better translates to "sicknesses" and the word *sorrows* better translates to "pains." This does not exclude the losses or hurts we go through in this life that cause us grief emotionally, but knowing this helps us understand the full scope of what Isaiah was prophesying.

Jesus carried not only our emotional traumas on the Cross, but our sicknesses and pains as well. If you are reading this and as you read you are suffering with an illness and dealing with pain, know that His blood decrees healing and deliverance from pain for you today! Believe it, declare it in Jesus' name!

FIFTH TIME

The fifth time Jesus' blood was shed was when they drove those spikes into His hands, nailing Him to the Cross. Words fail to express that unimaginable torment and excruciating pain our Lord suffered for us!

Hands speak of His work. His work was completed on the Cross! Now He sits at the right hand of the Father where He ever lives to make intercession for us as the Word says.

I believe that because His work was completed successfully, that through His power working in us and flowing through us, whatever we put our hands to can be successful also. Our work, our business, our ministries, and so forth. When we lay hands on people to pray for their healing, they can be healed because Jesus finished His work, His healing for us on the Cross.

Jabez, in 1 Chronicles 4:10 cried out to God a four-part prayer. We don't know very much about this man other than his name means "sorrow." Not a very positive moniker to have over you for life. Perhaps that is why he cried out to God. But this we do know, the Lord heard him and granted his request.

You can take the time to read the account in 1 Chronicles 4:10 (NIV), but one of the four things that he prayed is, *"Let your hand be with me."* When the hand of the Lord is upon you, with you, you are guaranteed victory because God's hand of enabling, strength, power, creativity, favor and more have rested on you and your outcome will be positive!

Scripture tells us that, *"The Lord was with Joseph so that he prospered..."* (Genesis 39:2 NIV). When the Lord is with you, that equals success! You + God = Success! As we read the account of Joseph's betrayal by his brothers (prophetically foreshadowing the Savior) and his being stripped of his coat of many colors (like Jesus was stripped to be beaten), being thrown into a pit (as the Savior was put in the grave, then descended into the pit of hell to take the keys from the devil), and being pulled out of the pit and eventually rising to be second in command at the right hand of Pharaoh (as Jesus ascended to the right hand of the Father where He intercedes for us), it's clear that the Lord's hand was on Joseph's life! When the Lord's hand is with us, He will bring us through all the snares of the wicked one and use our hands to deliver others by His power spoken by the blood of Jesus!

When we accept Jesus Christ as our Savior and the Lord of our lives, there's no doubt that the hand of the Lord rests on us, leading and guiding us, equipping us, strengthening us, providing for us, granting us favor and more. The blood that was shed from His hands paid for it. The blood decrees so!

SIXTH TIME

The sixth time Jesus' blood was shed was when they drove spikes into His feet securing Him to that "old rugged cross," as the songwriter wrote.

Feet speak of our walk. Although Jesus' earthly walk was only 33 years, with three being His ministry, He walked triumphantly as the Son of God, undeterred in His mission to pay the price for salvation, to reconcile God to man, and make a way for you and me to have access to the throne of Grace.

The apostle Paul told the church at Ephesus how to walk in what is now the fifth chapter of His epistle.

Walk in love. Ephesians 5:2 (NKJV): *"Walk in love, as Christ also has loved us and given Himself for us, an offering and a sacrifice to God for a sweet-smelling aroma."* Walking in love is sometimes easier said than done. With the indwelling power of the Holy Spirit, which was purchased by Jesus' blood, we can love the way Jesus loves us. None of us are worthy of His love! None of us deserve His lovingkindness, mercy, and grace. It was all bequeathed, left as an inheritance to us by the blood of Jesus, our Mediator (Hebrews 12:24). That blood decrees His love conquers, casts out fear, and enables us to walk in love for one another.

Walk as children of Light. Ephesians 5:8 (NKJV): *"For you were once darkness, but now are you are light in the Lord. Walk as children of light."* In the verses preceding, the apostle Paul describes many of the characteristics and actions of those who are not children of Light, but who rather walk in darkness. When the blood of Jesus washed your heart, He made you a new creation, and the things associated with darkness lost their appeal and hold on you. If you are struggling in any of these areas, know that the blood decrees freedom from bondage in the name of Jesus.

Walk circumspectly. Ephesians 5:15 (NKJV): *"See then that you walk circumspectly, not as fools, but as wise." Circumspectly* means to walk carefully, watching your step to avoid obstacles that might make you fall; it's as if you were entering a dark room without a flashlight, feeling your way through, avoiding hazards that might cause you to trip.

Walk in the Spirit. Ephesians 5:18-20 (KJV): *"And be not drunk with wine, wherein is excess; but be filled with the Spirit; speaking to yourselves in psalms and hymns and spiritual songs, singing and making melody in your heart to the Lord; giving thanks always for all things unto God and the Father in the name of our Lord Jesus Christ."*

Walk in victory. In Ephesians 5:18-21, Paul describes how to walk in victory over the flesh and live a life pleasing before the Lord.

Jesus walked all the way to Calvary in victory, so that you and I can walk all the way to glory in victory! Remember, because He overcame, so you and I overcome. We don't fight for victory; we fight from a position of victory—the victory of the Cross that the blood speaks over us. His blood says so!

This is only possible by the power of the Holy Spirit in us, empowering us to walk accordingly. The breath of the Spirit makes alive the power of the blood of Jesus to cause us to be what we could never be in our own strength. His blood declares it is possible.

SEVENTH TIME

The seventh time Jesus' blood was shed was when the Roman soldier thrust his spear into Jesus' side and blood and water gushed out. In that moment, just as the side of the first Adam in the garden of Eden was opened to create his wife, Eve, out of the side of the Second Adam, Jesus Christ, the church was born.

The bride of Christ, His church, will be with Him throughout all eternity. Upon Peter's confession *"thou art the Christ, the Son of the living God,"* Jesus proclaimed to him that *"upon this rock I will build my church, and the gates of hell shall not prevail against it."*

During Covid, many churches were pressured to not meet or gather, and when they did, there were strict seat-spacing guidelines that had to be followed. There is now strong reason to question the legitimacy of the need for these restrictions. What I do know is that the enemy knows that the church is powerful and that it has the backing of the blood of Jesus! It's no wonder that he would attempt to shut it down because he realizes there is power in our gathering together in the name of Jesus.

While I'm on the subject, although we are grateful for technology that has made it possible for online streaming of church services and for some this is the only way they can participate, there's no substitute for being together in His presence! Watching online will never take the place of what happens when the body of Christ comes together corporately. Someone has said that watching church services online is like watching a fireplace and the roaring fire on your television screen; you see it, but you don't feel the warmth.

Although there are some dismaying realities about the current condition of the present-day church, I do believe the Word when it says the church He comes back for will be a church *"without spot or wrinkle."* That can only mean that we are poised for a glorious, cleansing, perfecting, renewing revival that will sweep around the world preparing the bride for the Bridegroom's return.

In fact, we are seeing the beginnings of it already. A church that knows the Word of God, that believes its promises, prays and acts in faith believing His Word is true. A blood-bought, blood-washed, and a blood-speaking church that believes Hebrews 12:24, speaking accordingly.

There was popular song back in the '90s that I used to lead quite often in corporate praise titled, "Whose report will you believe?" It was inspired by the opening words of Isaiah 53. One line of the song says, "His report says I am healed…! Make no mistake, the report of the Lord, the Word of God, says the blood of Jesus, the Mediator speaks!" One of the *better things* it speaks and decrees is healing! Make the following declaration and believe God for a release of His healing power into your life.

DECREE

The blood of Jesus speaks healing to my body, my mind, my emotions, my spirit. I believe the Word of God that says, *"by His stripes we are healed,"* and I receive my healing now in the mighty name of Jesus—because the blood says so!

EIGHT

The Blood Decrees Deliverance

Deliverance is seen throughout the Bible, Old and New Testaments. From the Lord delivering righteous Lot from Sodom at the behest of his uncle Abraham, to Noah's family being spared from the judgment of the flood because of the wickedness that prevailed on the earth. From the Lord protecting His people during severe famine and drought by raising up Joseph (a type of Jesus, the Deliverer) to be second in command in Egypt, to the Lord delivering His chosen people from the grip of the Egyptians after many years of bondage by his servant Moses.

Deliverance is also seen in the Lord delivering His people from Babylonian captivity and restoring them to Jerusalem and the rebuilding of the temple, restoring temple worship; time after time He has proven Himself the Deliverer of His people.

Most importantly, the essence of the gospel is deliverance. *"God so loved the world that He gave His only begotten Son, that whoever believes in Him should not perish but have everlasting life"* (John 3:16 NKJV). In sending His Son Jesus, God made a way of deliverance for us. Colossians 1:13 (NKJV) says, *"He has delivered us from the power of darkness and conveyed us into the kingdom of the Son of His love."*

The New Testament mentions Jesus casting out evil spirits 55 times but only describes five of these events in detail. He cast demons out of a man in a synagogue (Mark 1) and two men near tombs (Matthew 8) and two more on other occasions.

All the examples I see of deliverance in the New Testament were done by Jesus and the apostles and were to individuals who were not what we would refer to as "born-again Christians." In the case of the maniac of Gadara, whose demons were cast into a herd of swine, this deliverance was obviously before the Lord was crucified, resurrected, and rose on the third day; it was before the Comforter, the Holy Spirit was poured out on the Day of Pentecost in the Upper Room. What is my point?

Jesus tells the disciples:

> And these signs shall follow them that believe; in my name shall they cast out devils; they shall speak with new tongues; they shall take up serpents; and if they drink any deadly thing, it shall not hurt them; they shall lay hands on the sick, and they shall recover (Mark 16:17-18 KJV).

These were all things that Christ followers would and should do. There is no inference here that indicates that those who needed to have devils cast out of them were Christians. In our day, and for the past several decades, deliverance has become a controversial topic and there is much confusion about it.

The question is often bantered about, "Can a Christian have a demon?" Or, "Can a Christian be demon-possessed?" I remember back when I was a Bible college student this was a much-discussed hot topic around this period of time. Christians needing deliverance became an accepted belief in many sectors of the church, particularly in charismatic circles.

I know it's not shared by all, but this is my opinion based on the subject from what I see in the Word. I feel I need to state it here, and I prayerfully ask that you consider it without immediately shutting down my argument.

In the Scripture passage in Mark 16, I see no indication that when Jesus says, *"shall they cast out devils"* it is referring to casting them out of believers who have the Spirit of the Lord in them.

How can a demon exist where the Spirit of the Lord exists? Is not the Spirit of the Lord greater than any demonic power? When He was on earth, He drove out demons with His Word. How much more will His presence (He is the Word) in our hearts dispel any power of darkness.

ALL THINGS HAVE BECOME NEW

I know the argument of those who do believe Christians can have a demon is that deliverance takes place in the soulish realm, not the spirit where the Holy Spirit dwells. I have an issue with that. The Word tells us in 2 Corinthians 5:17 that *"**old things** are passed away and behold **all things** have become new?"* Second Corinthians 5:17 means that when someone accepts Christ, their old life and sinful nature are considered *gone* and they are now a *new creation* with a fresh start, signifying a *complete transformation* and leaving behind the past.

I *do* believe that Christians can be *oppressed* by demons, for sure! I had a battle with this as a young Bible college student that almost derailed me from going into the ministry. More on that later. What brought me out of that dark period? The Word of God! The blood that speaks better things—things like deliverance over the power of the enemy.

You may disagree with me on this, but I challenge anyone who believes that Christians can have a demon to show me even one example of a Spirit-filled believer in the New Testament who was possessed by a demon and delivered. I don't believe you will find one.

Yes, there is a need for deliverance in the church. However, many would be delivered if they were taught and knew the Word of God. Many come from all sorts of backgrounds where they may have dabbled in occultic practices, witchcraft, and the like or have been caught up in lustful enticements that have brought bondage.

I strongly believe, however, in the power of the blood of Jesus to set people free from bondages of all kinds and that the Holy Spirit, once the blood has been applied at salvation, will through the Word bring about complete deliverance and liberty in Christ Jesus.

Those whom the Son sets free are free indeed. As John 8:36 (KJV) tells us, *"If the Son therefore shall make you free, ye shall be free indeed."* After all, the prophet Micah, who was a contemporary of the prophet Isaiah and also spoke prophetically of the Messiah, Jesus, called Him *"the breaker"* in Micah 2:13 (KJV). The following is the same verse in the Amplified Version of the Bible:

> The breaker [the Messiah, who opens the way] shall go up before them [liberating them]. They will break out, pass through the gate and go out; so their King goes on before them, the Lord at their head.

At the time this was prophesied and consequently recorded, it was speaking of the deliverance of the children of Israel who would be delivered from the grip of the Babylonians and Assyrians who had held them captive.

THE BREAKER ANOINTING

The Lord Jesus, the Messiah's anointing breaks through the barriers of the enemy and breaks off the limits of our own minds and ushers us into the *"exceedingly abundantly above all we ask or think"* realm (Ephesians 3:20). The "Breaker anointing" pushes back against the advances of the wicked one and causes the people of God to march forward in faith despite opposition.

Sadly, many in our society are held captive to addictions that they can't seem to break free from. What's even more disheartening is that many in the church also struggle with these devices of the devil. I truly believe that if they could grasp the power afforded to us by the blood of Jesus to deliver and set free, many would see the Breaker anointing "break every chain, break every chain, break every chain,"[2] as the modern worship song lyric says. The blood of Jesus decrees that the Breaker anointing delivers from the grip of the enemy!

Micah 2:13 has triple prophetic significance. Not only does it speak of the Lord's deliverance of the children of Israel, but it is a clear reference to the Lord Jesus Christ, the Messiah, who by His death, breaks us out of the bondage of sin and delivers us.

However, there will be one more time when the Breaker will break through the eastern skies and catch us away to be with Him eternally in glory.

---

2 "Break Every Chain," Jesus Culture, 2011.

This Breaker anointing, paid for by the blood of Jesus that speaks, is released through our mouths. Our words need to speak in agreement with what the blood speaks and in alignment with the "Ark of Testimony," and we will see breakthroughs accordingly. He has made a way for us through His precious blood that speaks.

I have the blessing of knowing personally Sinach, a worship artist out of Nigeria who wrote and made popular in worship the powerful song "Way Maker." I remember my first time hearing it and the impact it had on me. Thank you, Sinach, for being such a blessing to the body of Christ and reminding us that through Jesus' blood, the Breaker, He truly is our "Way Maker, Miracle Worker, Promise Keeper, Light in the darkness! That is who You are!"[3] The blood decrees it. The blood says so!

There's a powerful verse in Jeremiah that should be taught more often in my opinion. If believers could grasp its truth, they would less likely feel that they must be in a deliverance service to be set free. (Not that that doesn't happen or is essentially a negative.) However, the Word of the Breaker, Jesus, working in them can break any bondage of the wicked one. Jeremiah 23:29 (NIV) says, *"'Is not my word like fire,' declares the Lord, 'and like a hammer that breaks a rock in pieces?'"* According to Strong's Concordance, the word *rock* here means "a fortress or a stronghold." Yes, believers can certainly be up against strongholds of the enemy from time to time without question. Truthfully though, the Word (Jesus), who is described as a hammer here in this verse, can break each stronghold in pieces—can break the resistance of any demonic force that has come against God's people.

3 "Way Maker," Sinach, 2016.

ROMANS 8:26

Allow me to give you another powerful verse in the New Testament that reveals just how powerful our partnership with the Holy Spirit is over demonic powers and strongholds. It has for a long time been another one of my favorite verses, Romans 8:26. By the way, the entire chapter 8 in Romans is an essay on the work of the Holy Spirit in our hearts and lives, and we would do well to read it often. Romans 8:26 (KJV) says, *"Likewise the Spirit **helpeth** our infirmities: for we know not what we should pray for as we ought: but the Spirit itself maketh intercession for us with groanings which cannot be uttered."* Other translations translate the word *infirmities* as "weaknesses, corrupt desires, sickness, or troubles."

The word *helps* in Romans 8:26 is a long Greek word *sunantilambanomai,* pronounced "soon-an-tee-lam-ban-om-ahee," and it literally means "to take hold together." Together with whom? The Holy Spirit! Against what? The weakness, sickness, the frailty of body or spirit, the stronghold. This Scripture is saying we have the power, afforded to us by the blood of Jesus, to take hold together with the Holy Spirit and bring down any stronghold in the mighty name of Jesus! The blood says so!

Perhaps we need a little more teaching and preaching on how we have the power to be delivered by the partnership with the Holy Spirit, *taking hold together with Him against the stronghold* and less running to the most recently popular deliverance minister for a quick "deliverance." Most likely if the person has not learned how to cooperate with the Spirit and stay free from bondage, the deliverance will not last.

The more the Word of God dwells in us, the less any demonic power will be able to have power over us and the attempts of the devil will never stick because of the presence of the blood.

The blood of Jesus, His finished work on the Cross declares our deliverance! The blood says so! The blood decrees deliverance!

DECREE

The Lord Jesus paid for my deliverance from any form of bondage or addiction with His precious blood on Calvary. Today, I accept my privilege to partner with the Holy Spirit (Romans 8:26) and see the strongholds in my life brought down by the word of my testimony of what the blood speaks. His Word declares that whomever Jesus sets free is free indeed and I believe it! Today, I walk in the liberty wherewith He has set me free, and no chains of the enemy can keep me bound—because His blood says so!

NINE

The Blood Decrees a Seat at the King's Table

Tables are tremendously significant in the Word of God! I'm reminded of the story of how King David rescued Jonathan's son, Mephibosheth, from Lodebar in 2 Samuel chapter 9. By way of background, Mephibosheth's father, Jonathan, the son of King Saul—the first king of Israel who would eventually become possessed by an evil spirit and would turn on David—had a strong bound of friendship. In fact, David and Jonathan covenanted with each other (a common practice in that day) that if anything happened to one of them, they would assume responsibility for and take care of that friend's family as if their own.

Fast-forward years later and now both Saul and his son Jonathan have been killed, and David is now king over Israel. In keeping with the covenant he made with Jonathan, he inquires if there are any left of the household of Jonathan so as to fulfill his covenant with Jonathan, his friend.

Let's read the account in 2 Samuel 9 and draw some powerful insights from it; while doing so, see the Lord Jesus as the One who has rescued you and brought you to His table.

> David asked, "Is there anyone still left of the house of Saul to whom I can show kindness for Jonathan's sake?" Now there was a servant of Saul's household named Ziba. They summoned him to appear before David, and the king said to him, "Are you Ziba?" "At your service," he replied. The king asked, "Is there no one still alive from the house of Saul to whom I can show God's kindness?" Ziba answered the king, "There is still a son of Jonathan; he is lame in both feet." "Where is he?" the king asked. Ziba answered, "He is at the house of Makir son of Ammiel in Lo Debar" (2 Samuel 9:1-4 NIV).

Mephibosheth, now a grown man, had been dropped by a nurse and permanently disabled as a young child and caused him to become lame. At the time of David's inquiry, he's now been in this place called *Lo Debar* for some time. The meaning of *Lo Debar* in Hebrew is significant. *Debar* means "word," and the prefix *Lo* means "no." Together it means "no word" or "no thing." It also means "no pasture" because that aptly described this desolate place where Mephibosheth had been living.

Lo Debar, or Lodebar, represents the low places and seasons of our lives where we sometimes become stuck, like Mephibosheth, and need a deliverer to bring us out. When you're stuck in Lodebar, the Word of God seems like dead letters on the page and there's no *rhema* (the Word alive to your spirit) happening. It's a dry, lonely, and often discouraging place to be.

Upon hearing that Mephibosheth is in Lodebar, David sends the servant to go fetch him. Let's read it:

> So King David had him brought from Lo Debar, from the house of Makir son of Ammiel. When Mephibosheth

> son of Jonathan, the son of Saul, came to David, he bowed down to pay him honor. David said, "Mephibosheth!" "At your service," he replied. "Don't be afraid," David said to him, "for I will surely show you kindness for the sake of your father Jonathan. I will restore to you all the land that belonged to your grandfather Saul, and ***you will always eat at my table"*** (2 Samuel 9:5-7 NIV).

Here in this account, David prophetically represents the Lord Jesus who came to deliver us from our bondage and to free us from our "Lodebar." Once His presence came into our hearts, the Word of God became *rhema* to our spirits and brought life, liberty, and the abundance of the King's table.

Three observations from 2 Samuel 9:7: David says, "Don't be afraid, for I will surely **show you** kindness for the sake of your father Jonathan."

First, I believe that this Scripture wants us to understand that just as David showed Mephibosheth kindness, the Lord wants to give us a revelation of not only who He is, but what is available to us in His holy presence and at His table.

The Holy Spirit wants to give you and me a revelation of all that the blood of Jesus purchased for us and decrees over us, to understand that we have a seat at the King's table to partake of all His blessings. David treated Mephibosheth as if he were his own flesh and blood according to the covenant he made with his father, Jonathan. The Lord wants to remind us that we are His children because of His covenant; we belong to Him and have a right to all that His blood affords us at His table.

Second, David said to Mephibosheth that he would *"restore to you all the land that belonged to your grandfather Saul...."* There's restoration at the King's table provided for by the blood of the Lamb. No matter how awful our past, no matter how gross the sin, no matter how far we have strayed, there's restoration waiting for us in the King's presence. The blood says so! We don't have to linger in Lodebar permanently; the Lord, the Way Maker, our Promise Keeper, and Light in the darkness will make a way where there seems to be no way. Don't settle for Lodebar! Don't stay stuck! Accept the invitation to the King's table and partake of its bounty. God has a seat for you in His presence at His table that is loaded with benefits!

Third, David says to Mephibosheth in 2 Samuel 9:7 (NKJV), *"you shall eat bread at my table continually."* There's not only an invitation to come and sit at the table but the promise of bread; the bread of Heaven that truly satisfies and has no limit. I realize that the "prosperity gospel," as it's referred to, got way out of line scripturally, and I have been appalled at the gimmickry and manipulation that often accompanies its preaching. However, as the expression goes, "We mustn't throw out the baby with the bathwater."

Scripture is replete with promises of abundance in Christ Jesus; and yes, I do believe that means more than just our spiritual life. I believe that when we are in the presence of Jesus, His perfect *shalom* (well-being in every facet of your life) becomes available us, to you. That's not to say that at times we may not go through seasons of lack, but His death provides abundance for us, and God will supply *"all your need according to His riches in glory by Christ Jesus"* (Philippians 4:19 NKJV).

This story in 2 Samuel I believe prophetically demonstrates that one day soon the King, the Lord Jesus Himself, will break open the eastern sky and catch us up to His table. We will feast at the marriage supper of the Lamb. What a glorious day that will be! But for now, let's not forget what is available to us at the Lord's Supper. I believe the power of the blood is released, especially as we receive the Lord's Supper together.

The Greek word for *table* is *trapeza*. It can also be interpreted as "bank." When we come together in Jesus' name, when we participate in Communion, we are literally making a withdrawal from the bank of Heaven and can receive the fullness of the deposit Jesus made for us through His blood. His blood speaks that it's a "joint account." We can make withdrawals, because the blood says so!

If we could only realize the potential bounty that has been made available to us at the table of the Lord, I believe many more would be healed, delivered, and receive the abundance and riches of our salvation—all of which the blood of Jesus decrees!

In that glorious presence and communion with the Lord, His presence is loaded with all that the Lord has provided on the Cross and all our needs can be met. Let's take a look at some of the examples of what tables represent in the Word of God:

Tables speak of provision and abundance, as we've just seen in the story of David rescuing Mephibosheth and David bringing him to his table to eat continually. King David told Mephibosheth, *"you shall eat bread at my table continually."* There's continual supply, abundance, and provision at the table of the Lord for you and me today! The Lord wants us to remember that because of His sacrifice, His blood speaks a seat at His table forever. The table of the Lord, the King's table, is filled with His abundance.

I'm from Italian extraction as three of my grandparents were born in Italy, and the fourth, though born in America, had parents born in Italy also. Now it's no secret that Italians love to eat and they are known for their cuisine worldwide. I've had the blessing of traveling to Italy many times and enjoyed eating the best pasta, pizza, and various specialties of the "motherland." One thing is for sure, I never left the table hungry! There's always an abundance of food, or as the Italians say, *abondanza,* the Italian word for abundance. In Italian we also say, *Tutti a tavola e mangiare,* which means, "Everyone to the table and eat." They take that seriously, and believe me, I've accepted that invite to the table many times with pleasure!

There's a banquet prepared for us as believers at the King's table. In fact, one of the first things we will do after we are caught up in the air to ever be with the Lord is go to a feast—the marriage supper of the Lamb." Song of Soloman 2:4 (NKJV) prophetically refers to it: *"He brought me to the banqueting house, and His banner over me was love."* The love of the Lord, demonstrated by coming to die for us on the Cross, provided a seat at His table where we can feast continually of His abundance. That blood says come and eat.

We often hear the verse Psalm 65:11 (NKJV) quoted or see images pictured for us at the beginning of a new year. It says, *"You crown the year with Your goodness, and Your paths drip with abundance."* The Hebrew word used here for *abundance* is the word *deshen*. According to Strong's Concordance: "Definition: Fatness, abundance, fertility, ashes (of sacrifices); Meaning: the fat, fatness, abundance, the, ashes of sacrifices."

David, in speaking of the Lord's goodness and abundance, is reflecting on the sacrifices that the priests would make on behalf of Israel. After slaying the animal, the sacrifice would be burnt. What is the final state of anything burnt? Ashes. When the ashes appeared on the altar, it was a sign to all Israel that the work was finished.

Ashes spoke prophetically of the completed work of Jesus, the perfect sacrificial Lamb who was slain on the Cross, and when He cried, *"It is finished,"* the work was completed. The price was paid in blood for us to live in abundance spiritually, physically, emotionally, and the other aspects of our lives because of the favor of God. That blood decrees abundance.

Whenever the devil presents a lack to you, whether financially or a lack of healing for a physical ailment or a lack of resolution of a relationship conflict or whatever it may be, answer him back by declaring, "Ashes!" Remind him that the work was done on Calvary! Remind him that the blood speaks provision and that our God has promised to abundantly supply all our needs (Philippians 4:19). That there is no lack in the Lord God! Because the blood says so!

Tables speak of protection. David says in Psalm 23:5 (NKJV), *"You prepare a table before me in the presence of my enemies...."* God's promise, spoken by the blood of His Son Jesus, is protection. David also says in Psalm 3:3 (NKJV), *"But You, O Lord, are a shield for me, My glory and the One who lifts up my head."* In the verses preceding, David mentions how his enemies are increasing and have risen up against him having caused great trouble and despair. What a glorious truth this is! The glory of the Lord, His presence, is a divine shield protecting and shielding us from any attempts of the destroyer, the devil! The blood decrees it!

Tables speak of healing and being made whole. Jesus, on the night before He was crucified, took bread and broke it saying, *"This is my body which is given for you."* Luke 22 goes on to say, *"Likewise also the cup after supper, saying, 'This cup is the new testament* *in my blood, which is shed for you,"* (Luke 22:19-20 KJV). That holy meal was prophetic of the Lord's death that provides healing for our brokenness in every way. Just as Isaiah prophesied, *"with His stripes we were healed."*

Notice that Jesus says to the disciples, *"This cup is the new testament in my blood."* What is a testament? The word *testament* is defined as: "something that serves as tangible proof or evidence, a statement of belief, a credo, a usually formal written directive providing for the disposition of one's property after death; a will." Jesus' blood decrees His statement, to us who believe, His "providing for the disposition of one's (His) property after (His death); a (His) will."

This New Covenant in His blood, this Testament, is another clear indication that that blood testifies, that blood speaks, that blood decrees healing and deliverance!

Tables speak of revelation. Do you know the story of the two men on the road to Emmaus recorded for us in Luke chapter 24? It's the day of the Resurrection and these two men were walking and talking about the Lord on their way to the village of Emmaus. A third Man joins them and walks with them, listening to their conversation. He begins conversing with them also. Something about this Man's presence caused them to want Him to stay with them. Scripture tells us that this third Man, none other than the resurrected Lord Jesus Himself, made as if He was going to leave them as it was almost dusk. The Bible tells us in Luke 24:29 (NIV), *"they urged him strongly,"* saying, *"Stay with us...."* This is a powerful key to a deeper walk with the Lord—learn how to constrain Him, urge Him to come to your house in worship and prayer and He will do as He did with these two travelers on the road to Emmaus and visit you with His presence.

The story goes on to tell us that Jesus acquiesced and went with them to their house. As they sat for a meal, broke bread, most likely their table, the moment they began to eat, they realized that the One whom they had in their company was no ordinary man but the Son of the Living God, Jesus Christ crucified and risen just as He had said. Scripture tells us so dramatically in Luke 24: 31 (NKJV), *"Then their eyes were opened and they knew Him; and He vanished from their sight."* In other words, they had a revelation of Him; they recognized He was the Lord Jesus.

Every time we obey the Lord's Word and *"Do this in remembrance of Me,"* we have an opportunity to have our eyes opened, to know Him and receive a revelation of Him (Luke 22:19).

There's revelation at the table of the Lord! The blood decrees it!

Tables speak of revival! In that same account in Luke 24, after Jesus had vanished from them, verse 32 tells us, *"And they said one to another, 'Did not our heart burn within us while He talked with us on the road, and while He opened the Scriptures to us?'"* That burning in their hearts was revival fire! There's revival at the table of the Lord.

Tables speak communion with the Lord. There's communion at the table of the Lord. There's a reason we call partaking of the Lord's supper Communion. Perhaps we have not realized due to tradition or lack of teaching that when we obey the Lord's command, we have an opportunity to commune with Him. Our Catholic friends believe that the elements of the Eucharist literally become the body and blood of Jesus when they are observing this holy ordinance, derived from the words that Jesus spoke, *"This is My body."* I believe Jesus was saying that when you remember Me in taking Communion, My Holy Spirit in you will make my death and resurrection real to you, and the Holy Spirit will distribute to you all the benefits of the Cross. You will become aware of My glorious presence in so doing.

Hebrews tells us Jesus died *"once and for all."* To believe that the elements physically become the body and blood of Jesus would mean a violation of His Word in Hebrews. The price for sin was paid once and for all. The price for our healing and deliverance was paid once and for all, there's no "to be continued." It is done! It is finished!

A Lodebar Deliverance

Getting back to the story of David rescuing Mephibosheth and bringing him to his table, allow me to share a testimony that is so inspiring. It happened several years ago while I was ministering in the northern part of Maine. You will be blessed by it, I assure you; more importantly, I believe it will cause you to stretch out your faith and believe God for your own personal deliverance from what "Lodebar" you are experiencing right now.

Several years ago I was invited to be the guest speaker at the Whited Bible Camp in Presque Isle, Maine. One night I preached this message from 2 Samuel 9 about Lodebar. I wasn't aware that a wonderful local pastor was in attendance and that he had suffered for many years with crippling pain from a leg injury caused in a horrific car accident years earlier. He had had multiple surgeries but still no relief for the chronic, agonizing pain.

After I preached, as is my custom, we began to worship, and the word of knowledge began to operate through me. I remember hearing the Holy Spirit say, which I repeated, "There's a pastor here who has suffered for many years with leg pain, and today the Lord wants to *fetch* you from your Lodebar and heal you." To my right a man haltingly stood up and signaled that he was that man.

I asked him to come forward and tell me his problem. He briefly described the torment he had been in for many years because of the car accident years before. As I always do, I asked him, "Do you believe the Lord can heal you right now?" to which he responded, "Yes, absolutely." We laid hands on him and prayed as the Scripture declares we can do, and all glory to the Lord, the pain left his body, and he straightened up, standing tall which he hadn't been able to do in years!

Glory to God. The next day, my wife and I decided that since we were so close to Canada, we'd take a road trip to beautiful Prince Edward Island to relax for a day or two before going home. While driving, my cell phone rang, and it was the wife of the pastor who had to share what happened when her husband stepped into the pulpit that following Sunday. They sent us the pictures of that awful car accident years earlier and of him in the hospital all bandaged up and in traction. Mind you, his congregation had only seen him hunched over and gripping the pulpit in pain while preaching. Oh yes, he'd been in his own Lodebar for a long, long time!

The pastor and his wife decided that rather than both coming into the sanctuary at the same time, as they usually did, that she would go in first and open the service, lead some worship, and then he would step out into the sanctuary. The moment he walked through the door, and they saw their pastor walking upright and effortlessly without pain, the place exploded with rejoicing and praise broke out throughout the whole congregation. When he gave his testimony of how the Lord had healed him, healing began to break out in the congregation as well, and many were healed that morning! Glory to God!

Decree

In Christ Jesus, I've been rescued from Lodebar. Lord, you see where I am right now! You see that I in my own strength or power do not have the ability to move forward—but Your blood speaks my rescue today. I do not have to stay in this low place or season without revelation of Your Word and without receiving all that is mine and all that Your blood decrees over me. I embrace all the table of the Lord offers me—His abundance and provision for every aspect of my life; His protection from the enemy; His healing for my body, soul, mind, and spirit; revelation of Him through His Word; revival and spiritual renewal because the blood says so!

Today, I decree that I accept the standing invitation spoken by His blood to be delivered by the Holy Spirit to leave Lodebar and never return there! I am taking my place at the King's table, because the blood says so!

TEN

THE BLOOD DECREES PEACE

THE SHALOM OF THE LORD

John 20:21-22 (NIV) says, "*Again Jesus said, 'Peace be with you! As the Father has sent me, I am also sending you.' And with that he breathed on them and said, 'Receive the Holy Spirit.'*"

Peace, my friend, is part of our inheritance in Christ Jesus. He is the Prince of Peace (Isaiah 9:6) and the fruit of His presence in our hearts is peace. Whatever you are facing now, let the Lord breathe His peace into your being right now as you are reading this book and claim what's rightfully yours in Christ.

I don't think it's an accident that just before Jesus breathed on the disciples to receive the Holy Spirit, He blessed them with the words *"Peace be with you."* There is a strong correlation between the breath of God (the blessing of the Spirit) in your life and the realization of His perfect peace. The very presence of God's breath in you produces a peace that cannot be produced by any other means.

You have probably heard it taught, but just in case, let me point out that there are two types of peace that we receive when we accept and receive the Lord Jesus Christ into our hearts. They are the peace *with* God and the peace *of* God. There is no peace *of* God without peace *with* God!

Peace with God is ours when we accept the perfect sacrifice of His Son, Jesus, on the Cross and believe on Him as our Savior. It is our righteous standing with God, our position in Christ, that has been reconciled, restored, and purchased by the blood of Jesus, which speaks it is ours! It's the peace of knowing that all is well with our souls and our standing before God, and we no longer must hide in fear of His judgment because the penalty has been paid in full by His Son and appropriated to our hearts through faith.

The separation that was caused by man's sin in the Garden of Eden was reconciled when Jesus became our peace offering, when He willingly humbled Himself and became obedient to the Cross. Philippians 2:8 (NIV) says, *"And being found in appearance as a man, he humbled himself by becoming obedient to death—even the death on a cross!"*

Jesus' supreme act of humility paid the price for us to be brought near to God as Ephesians 2:13 (NKJV) tells us: *"But now in Christ Jesus you who once were far off have been brought near by the blood of Christ."* The blood of Jesus brings us near to God. In other words, back into His glorious presence where there is no condemnation, no fear of judgment, no separation because of sin, thereby giving us peace with God.

However, there's a second kind of peace that is ours as part of the blessing of Abraham. It becomes ours as a divine result of peace with God coming to our hearts: the peace *of* God. Without peace with God, it is impossible to experience the peace of God!

"Peace [shalom] *I leave with you, My peace I give to you; not as the world gives do I give I to you. Let not your heart be troubled, neither let*

it be afraid" (John 14:27 NKJV). *Shalom* is the Hebrew word used here translated into English as *peace*.

When Jesus said these amazing words to the disciples, He had just finished teaching them about the Holy Spirit, the Comforter, whom He said He would ask the Father to give them after He was taken up back into Heaven to prepare a place for them. Here again, we see a strong correlation between the Holy Spirit's presence in the believer's life and the presence of peace.

The word *shalom* is power-packed! Let me share with you the revelation of what it means in the heart and life of you and me as Christians, or Christ followers.

There are a couple of observations I'd like to draw your attention to about the word *peace (shalom)* that the Lord Jesus uses in this familiar passage of Scripture in John 14:27. If you visit Israel, as I have on numerous occasions, you will often be greeted by the locals with the word *"Shalom."* It is a common greeting used in much the same way as we here in the US say hello and good-bye or as the Italians say the word *"Ciao."* (I had to throw that in there because of my Italian heritage.) However, shalom is much more than just a common greeting—much, much more in fact!

I have heard rabbis and Hebrew scholars teach about *shalom* and even everyday Orthodox Jews will tell you the same thing: when you say, "Peace" or "Shalom," the Hebrew word that Jesus spoke to them, you are pronouncing a blessing on that person, and their entire family for that matter. The word *peace* isn't just a relaxed state of mind either, not by any means!

The word *shalom* means *total well-being*—not just your mind, but also your body, soul, spirit, and every facet of your life! When the blood of Jesus decrees peace, peace floods your heart and life, and you are truly blessed with the shalom blessing of His peace in your total being. No part of you is lacking or left unaffected by it because the Prince of Peace is living inside you, breathing His blessing into every aspect of your life; the blood speaks peace to us. This includes your marriage, your finances, your business dealings, your health also!

The "Blessing of Abraham" is part of your birthright as a believer in Christ Jesus and as a child of Abraham! In Hebrew tradition, the birthright was a blessing passed on from a father to his eldest male child just prior to his death. I will elaborate more on that later; but for now, just know that it is part of your inheritance as the firstborn in Jesus Christ and is for you and your household and the generations that follow. We know that because Jesus says, *"My peace I leave with you."* The word *leave* here in Hebrew is the connotation of someone who bequeaths or leaves an estate or an inheritance to his loved ones after he or she passes.

Jesus wants us to know that He has left for us or bequeathed to us His shalom blessing in every dimension of our life because the Comforter, the Holy Spirit, the Spirit of the Lord, is residing in us. I like to think of it this way: the Father left us His will, purchased by the Son and distributed by the Executor of the Will, the Holy Spirit. It's the Spirit of the Lord who blesses us with the shalom blessing of the Lord and imparts it to us as we need it.

In our household growing up, and even throughout our adult lives, we have often used the expression "All is well" when we were facing a trying or difficult situation that had presented itself and was challenging our faith. The phrase comes from the story of the Shunamite woman in 2 Kings 4, who when the prophet Elisha asked if all was well with her, her husband and child, she replied, "All is well." That was quite the statement since her son had just died. She came in faith believing that after her visit with the prophet Elisha, all would be well. My dad used the phrase when there was a crisis in our household.

I believe it started after my dad, who was a carpenter by trade, fell off a steep roof and broke all his ribs. Miraculously, his life was spared and with the extra insurance money after the medical bills had been paid, he purchased a piano for my mom who was a wonderful pianist. It was on that piano that my twin brother John and I learned how to play the piano and would eventually be the launching of our adult musical careers and ministry!

When Dad's accident happened, my mom wondered where their income would come from and how she was going to feed and clothe their four young, growing boys. Dad, who had great faith and who always possessed a disposition of peace, said to her, "Don't worry, Mom, all is well!" And you know what? It was! He soon recovered and returned to the job he had been working on.

When one job would end, almost without fail, he'd get another call to begin a new one that would last for several weeks or months, and the Lord provided repeatedly in that manner. That little phrase, "All is well," stuck, and we used it over and over and often when we faced adversity as a family. We weren't being superficial or insincere, it was just our way of reminding each other our faith was anchored in the fact that our Lord Jesus' presence in our lives, family, and household would see us through the storm—and that in the end, His shalom peace and blessing would work everything out for our eventual good, no matter how bad things seemed now.

It's important to speak what the blood speaks! In doing so, we were saying shalom without using the word and pronouncing the blessing on each other and the circumstances at hand knowing the Prince of Peace would reign supreme over all the affairs of our lives.

Out of the Valley of Despair

What I'm about to share with you is very personal. However, I feel I must share it for those who may be going through a similar battle with fear or experiencing oppressive thoughts that the adversary, the devil, has been harassing you with. The blood speaks God-given peace. I can say with confidence and from personal experience that there is a way out of your valley of despair and God can and will bring you out victoriously. He will deliver you and bring you out by His power!

Here's why I know this to be true.

Back when I was a freshman in Bible college, I went through a devastating experience with fear that almost derailed my life and the ministry that the Lord had for me to accomplish. Without exaggeration, for a time I feared I was losing my mind, and the devil as much as whispered that lie often to me during that horrible season in my life. It seemed out of nowhere, I was attacked by a spirit of fear, and it literally crippled me to the point that I had to call my parents and ask them to come and get me and take me home.

Prior to that, I had never experienced fear like this and had enjoyed a normal, happy childhood. I had the blessing of being born into a godly family with a heritage of faith and had been filled with the Holy Spirit at the age of 12. In fact, my baptism in the Holy Spirit was so glorious that for hours afterward, I couldn't speak in English but spoke in the heavenly language that the Lord had given me. In 1968, evangelist David DeMola came to hold revival services at my home church in Nutley, New

Jersey. During the two weeks of the revival, many of the young people in our church had been filled with the Holy Spirit. I was spiritually hungry to experience the same glory and infilling of the Holy Spirit, and I was getting discouraged because it had not happened to me yet.

I remember clearly that on the Sunday morning—the last day of the revival—when Pastor DeMola gave the altar call for those who wanted to receive the baptism of the Holy Spirit. I went forward quickly with many of my fellow youth who prayed earnestly with me to receive. In that service, all of a sudden, foreign words began coming to my mind and I began to speak them out, though with some hesitation and faltering.

Pastor DeMola, being very wise, counseled me not to be satisfied with that but to come back that night, and he prophetically spoke that the Lord would fill me to overflowing in the evening service. That is exactly what happened. I returned that evening and once again, when the altar appeal was given, I went forward and began seeking the Lord with all my heart. Suddenly I was overcome by the presence of the Spirit of the Lord, and I began to praise and speak in a fluent language that continued for hours. It was as if a well of Living Water was erupting from deep within me—an experience I will never forget! I was gloriously filled with the Spirit. It was then that I knew my life had a calling on it for fulltime ministry, and I left for Zion Bible College just a few years later.

Back to the Bible college experience. I remember how excited my twin brother, John, and I were when we arrived on campus in the fall of 1972 to begin our college life. Everything was going along great until, as I said earlier, this horrible attack began.

THE LIAR LIES

Then, suddenly my mind was attacked with the most vile, horrible thoughts and the enemy began to tell me viscous lies that literally shut me down and paralyzed me. He said things like, "You aren't really a Christian. You have blasphemed the Holy Ghost. You will never make it in ministry. You will never be married or have children. You will end up committing suicide," and much worse things that I don't care to repeat. I was so devastated by it that I couldn't even think straight, let alone go to classes and continue studying. It comforted me years later to learn that other men of God who were called to impact the world went through similar experiences. Satan will do everything he can to rob us of our peace, and in so doing, try to thwart the plan of God for our lives. He's a liar and was defeated when Jesus cried, *"It is finished"* and forever secured perfect peace for us that day on Calvary.

Did you know that the name for the devil in Greek is *diabolos*. *Diabolos:* devil, accuser, slanderer. It literally means "to cast, or hurl, or to strike." That's exactly what the devil does against the Christian. He strikes over and over at our minds, hurling his lies and accusations at us to wear us down both mentally, spiritually, and physically with his charges, lies, and thoughts contrary to the Word of God and contrary to what Jesus' blood decrees over us. Remember! The battlefield for spiritual warfare takes place in the mind. He's very good at hurling his demonic suggestions and assaults at us, and if we are not aware of what the Word of God declares and what the blood of Jesus decrees over us, we can succumb to his fear and tactics and lose faith.

The believer who is strong and mature in Christ is not ignorant of his devices but is fully aware of his tactics and knows how to stand strong against the attack of the wicked one.

Thankfully, I had a mom and dad who understood spiritual warfare and came quickly to my aid. Mom drove up to Rhode Island from New Jersey to pick me up and take me home for a while, and they began teaching me how to stand against the wicked one and his lies and how to do battle in the spirit realm. I remember my dad saying, "Jim, the devil is like a big dog who at first seems ferocious when it is charging toward you. Most often, if you stand still, he will come up to you, sniff around a little and then run off because he will sense that you are not afraid of him."

Not to say that the devil does not have power, but often, "his bark is bigger than his bite," and the Word says he comes *"as a roaring lion seeking whom he may devour"* to scare us and put us in the bondage of fear. We must stand against him *"in the power of God's might"* and the Word then declares as we resist him, he will flee from us. This kind of resistance is not just mental, it is only possible when *"the Spirit of the Lord will lift up a standard against him"* (Isaiah 59:19 NKJV) and he realizes he's no match for the Lord!

Mom spoke to me many powerful passages of Scripture including, *"No weapon formed against you shall prosper, and every tongue that rises against you in judgment you shall condemn"* (Isaiah 54:17 NKJV) and 2 Corinthians 10:5 (NKJV), which says, *"Casting down arguments and every high thing that exalts itself against the knowledge of God, and bringing into captivity every thought to the obedience of Christ"*—and that spirit of fear eventually left me.

Little by little, as I began to speak the Word of God and pray in the Spirit in the tongue He had given me several years earlier, I began to become stronger in my inner man and was able to resist the devil's wicked thoughts and lies—and the peace of God began to fill my heart and mind. It was during this period as I spent time in the Lord's presence, He breathed into my spirit and it defeated the spirit of fear that had crippled me. It took several weeks, but praise be to the Lord, I not only completed my freshman year of college, I eventually graduated and even continued on to earn bachelor's degrees in music and in Bible Literature.

Take That, Devil!

From that time until now, that fear has never returned, and I have learned that when you stand in your position of authority in Christ and use His Word, which is a mighty sword against the enemy, you become equipped with divine, supernatural strengthening and your heart is no longer fearful. Satan is a liar! It takes the breath of God's Spirit, though, to make the Word of God *rhema* to your spirit and cause you to utilize your weapons of warfare against the enemy.

Just to shame the devil and prove him to be the liar that he is, that horrible experience was over 49 years ago. Since then, I have been in full-time ministry for more than 49 years, traveled millions of miles around the world, ministered in over 90 countries, stood in front of millions of people sharing the saving, healing gospel of Jesus Christ, have been married to my beautiful wife, Mindy for almost 40 years, and am a father of an awesome son, Daniel, who is now 36 and married to a lovely, Christian lady named Linsey. Take that, devil! I have experienced the blessing of peace that comes to life when God's Spirit is living and breathing inside. I realized that the blood decrees peace!

My friend, do not allow the spirit of fear to control you or destroy the abundant life that God has promised you: the blood decrees peace. Peace is part of your inheritance as a child of Abraham. Peace is the fruit of God's presence. The Lord left it for you when He said, *"My peace give I to you"* (John 14:27), so take what is rightfully yours today.

In the many years that have followed that horrible experience, I have often used the lessons I learned during that time and know how to stand in the authority Christ has given us believers.

If I had succumbed to the spirit of fear and not realized my position in Christ Jesus *"far above all principality and powers,"* I would have forfeited an amazing tenure of ministry and many of the awesome blessings the Lord had in store me in my life.

PEACE, BE STILL

Do you know the New Testament story of when Jesus and the disciples got into a boat on the Sea of Galilee and a massive storm arose? The story is recorded for us in the Gospel of Matthew 8:23-27 and Mark 4:35-41. The disciples began to panic and clamor, fretting for their lives and safety—and what was the Lord doing? He was sleeping! Despite the dangerous problem that had suddenly arisen, Jesus was calmly sleeping in the boat as if oblivious to the situation. In response to the men's turmoil and questioning if He cared about their welfare, Jesus simply said, *"Peace, be still!"*

How often do we have the same reaction to the storms that come our way—and Jesus' response is still the same today! *"Peace, be still!"* When Jesus said these amazing words to the disciples, He was assuring them that He was aware of the crisis, but to be still (let Him handle it). Because His presence was with them, they could rest in knowing that everything was going to be all right in the end!

We read the account of this story in Mark 4:35-41 (NKJV), which says:

> On the same day, when evening had come, He said to them, "Let us cross over to the other side." Now when they had left the multitude, they took Him along in the boat as He was. And other little boats were also with Him. And a great windstorm arose, and the waves beat into the boat, so that it was already filling. But He was in the stern, asleep on a pillow. And they awoke Him and said to Him, "Teacher, do You not care that we are perishing?" Then He arose and rebuked the wind, and said to the sea, "Peace, be still!" And the wind ceased and there was a great calm. But He said to them, "Why are you so fearful? How is it that you have no faith?" And they feared exceedingly, and said to one another, "Who can this be, that even the wind and the sea obey Him!"

The word *peace* that Jesus uses when He rebuked the wind and the waves saying, *"Peace, be still"* is a different word for peace in Hebrew. It is the word *shathaq,* which means "be still or be quiet." Jesus may not only have been speaking to the wind and the waves but also to disciples who were making a lot of noise in their frantic response to the violent storm rather than realizing that the One who controls the wind and the waves was in the boat with them—and because of His presence, everything would turn out all right!

How much like them are we when a crisis or a storm in life comes our way? Rather than trust in the fact that He, the Lord, is with us "in our boat," so to speak, right there with the authority over everything including sickness, death, hell, and the grave, we panic and get ourselves all worked up into a frenzied state, even questioning as the disciples did when they asked, *"Do You not care that we are perishing?"*

That is why we must hide the Word of God in our hearts so that when the storms arise, when the difficult or even impossible situations come our way, the Holy Spirit can "bring back to our remembrance" the truths of the Word and apply them to our hearts and minds, bringing perfect peace right there in the middle of the storm. Jesus has not left us defenseless; His blood decrees peace that passes all understanding to come to our aid in our moments of crisis. We can speak "Peace, be still" to the storms of life, and they will subside just as the waves of the Sea of Galilee did at the sound of His voice and His command.

His Peace

You might wonder when reading this famous passage, as I did prior to my many tours of the Holy Land, how can a storm come up in minutes on the "sea" of Galilee when it's actually a huge lake? You see, that lake is situated beneath the intersection of two great mountain chains that form a wind tunnel that directly blows over the Sea of Galilee. When storms blow from the north, the wind picks up and is funneled down through the valley between the two mountains, and literally in minutes a gigantic storm can erupt on the Sea of Galilee. This is just one of the many, many examples of how visiting the Holy Land will breathe new life into your Bible reading and comprehension of how the geography and culture of the day give you understanding of the many things that Jesus taught and did in His earthly ministry.

One last truth I'd like to bring to your attention before concluding this section on the blood decrees peace is this. Notice that after Jesus said, *"Peace I leave with you, my peace I give unto you…."*

He said, ***"Let not** your heart be troubled, neither **let** it be afraid"* (John 14:27 KJV). The word *let* is a word of permission. In other words, Jesus was saying you have the power to either give permission for fear to control your heart and mind and consequently your life, or to *not let* it do so by standing in your supernaturally given authority and power to speak to the storm as He did, and command it to "Be still." Remember that just as Jesus was with the disciples in their hour of need in that horrific storm on the Sea of Galilee, He is in you to provide His perfect *shalom,* total well-being to your mind, body, spirit, and to every facet of your life, including your finances and relationships. He is with you also to speak, "Peace, be still" in your hour of despair.

Dear reader, I encourage you to pause right now and speak to the storm in your life, that thing that tries to bring fear to your heart and mind, the tempest that rages at you trying to take your eyes off the One who calms the storms in your life—Jesus.

The blessing of peace is yours; it is part of your inheritance. As a child of God, take your peace by faith and claim your inheritance today that the blood decrees. As Jesus says, *"Let not your heart be troubled, neither let it be afraid."* Starting today, walk in the blood-bought promise of peace that is yours because the blood says so!

Remind yourself that you come from a heritage of faith and a long line of believers who have trusted in the God of our Father Abraham and just as He blessed them in every dimension of their lives with His shalom peace, He will bless you also and the generations that follow you.

DECREE

Today, I recognize that the Prince of Peace is living in my heart by the Holy Spirit. I take the fruit of His peace, His perfect peace,

His shalom that passes all understanding, in Jesus' name. I will not *let,* or allow, the enemy of my soul to cause my heart to be troubled, fearful, or anxious. I walk in His perfect love that casts out all fear—because the blood says so.

ELEVEN

The Blood Decrees Recovery and Restoration

Has something ever been stolen from you? It's a very violating experience; and after you get over the shock of the loss, anger can set in for the thief!

When I was a young boy growing up in New Jersey, we had a family get-together at our house, which was on one end of our charming town of Nutley. Our relatives on Mom's side of the family lived across town from where my mom had grown up. The city of Nutley is a lovely town, located about 30 minutes outside New York City. In fact, when I was growing up, I could see the New York skyline from my bedroom window.

As the party was wrapping up and some of the family members had left, we were cleaning up the kitchen (always lots of food involved in an Italian family gathering), and the phone rang. I answered the phone, which was hanging on the wall in our kitchen, and I heard my Aunt Esther exclaim, "We've been robbed!" She had just returned to her home from being at our party.

I remember the feeling that went through me hearing those words, partly because as a child, things make a big impact on you and partly because of my concern for my dear aunt and uncle and their family. I can still remember the anxiety in her voice to this day. Thankfully, even though the thieves took a few valuables, none of the family was home at the time and no one was harmed, other than being emotionally shaken up. (Dear Aunt Esther went to be with the Lord just this past year after living a long life until the age of 96, and believe me, she knew a thing or two about recovery and restoration!)

Robbery

David, the psalmist, knew a thing or two about what it feels like to have been robbed!

The psalmist David, who became king of Israel went through a terrifying experience of loss; and to make matters worse, not only David but all his soldiers who had been away with him doing battle also lost their wives, children, and all of their belongings when the Amalekites invaded their city, plundered it, and burned it to the ground. The chilling story is described in 1 Samuel 30. Thankfully, this story has a happy ending!

> Now it happened, when David and his men came to Ziklag, on the third day, that the Amalekites had invaded the South and Ziklag, attacked Ziklag and burned it with fire, and had taken captive the women and those who were there, from small to great; they did not kill anyone, but carried them away and went their way. So David and his men came to the city, and there it was, burned with fire; and their wives, their sons, and their daughters had been taken captive. Then David and the people who were with him lifted up their voices

> and wept, until they had no more power to weep. And David's two wives, Ahinoam the Jezreelitess, and Abigail the widow of Nabal the Carmelite, had been taken captive. Now David was greatly distressed, for the people spoke of stoning him, because the soul of all the people was grieved, every man for his sons and his daughters.... (1 Samuel 30:1-6 NKJV).

The loss was so great, as it would be for anyone faced with such a devastating experience, that although David and the soldiers had been mighty and strong in battle, these grown men cried until they had no tears left to cry! Have you ever been there? I have and it's not pleasant! Imagine, David was not only grieving over his own personal loss of his wives, but on top of this, his men turned on him and were so angry that they were talking about killing him!

After you get over the emotional impact and shock of going through such an immeasurable loss, you have only two options: 1) stay stuck in the loss and its impact on you, which leads to a deeper state of depression; or 2) get angry with the enemy that has inflicted the loss, pick yourself up, regroup, and go after what has been stolen, taking back what is rightfully yours! This is exactly what God told David to do!

I'm not advocating that anyone go after the "people" who have wronged you, but rather get angry at the source, the wicked one, who according to the Word in John 10:10 has come *"to steal, and to kill, and to destroy!"* Sometimes you just have to say to yourself, "Enough is enough; I'm taking back my stuff!" When the Spirit of the Lord comes on you, you rise in holy anger against the plots of the devil to destroy you or your family and begin to take back what has been stolen. This, my friend, is also one of the *better things* that the blood of Jesus decrees to us: restoration and recovery.

"How do I do that?" you ask. By doing what David did. "What did he do?" The answer is found in the last sentence in 1 Samuel 30:6, *"David strengthened himself in the Lord his God."*

DAVID'S FIVE KEYS

Let's look in detail at five keys that David used to strengthen himself in the Lord.

KEY 1: STRENGTHEN YOURSELF IN THE LORD IN GOD'S PRESENCE

In times of loss, the first thing to do is to strengthen yourself in the Lord as David did. We do that in several ways. Notice the Scripture says David *"strengthened himself."* When we experience heartache, loss, and hardship, our first reaction is often to run to others for comfort, consolation, and encouragement, which is good to a certain extent. Thank God for caring people who are there for us in our hour of need. However, nothing can take the place of knowing how to *"come boldly to the throne of grace, that we may obtain mercy and find grace to help in time of need"* (Hebrews 4:16 NKJV).

Learn how to get into God's presence. Allow His Spirit to breathe recovery into your spirit, which will give you a renewing in your body, mind, and spirit, enabling you to pick yourself up along with all the shattered pieces of your life and go after what has been stolen. In His presence, He will reveal His plan and His promises about your future: *"'For I know the plans I have for you,' declares the Lord, 'plans to prosper you and not to harm you, plans to give you hope and a future'"* (Jeremiah 29:11 NIV).

After I launched into my new season of ministry in 2010—although I knew the Lord was in it and was definitely fulfilling what He had spoken to me about several years earlier in 2003 about Him bringing me into a new season of ministry—I went through a very tough time emotionally because of the loss of something I had cherished for more than 22 years of my life.

It was painful to have taken away from me, quite suddenly, my position, my work associates who were more like a second family, and my livelihood and source of income in a matter of days. I felt as though I was experiencing a death, so to speak, and was grieving just as one does when a loved one passes. Yes, I will admit it! I cried and wept over the loss like David and his men, *"until there were no more tears left."* But, thankfully, I had learned over the years how to strengthen myself as David did, and the first place I ran to was the presence of the Lord.

For about the first three months of 2010 I experienced the comfort and fellowship of the Spirit in a glorious way each day as I would spend hours in prayer and reading the Word of God. Out of that painful time came glorious revelations of the Word and I wouldn't trade that for anything. Not only that, but He breathed faith back into my spirit to believe that as painful as it was to let go of what had been dear to me, if I trusted Him and stepped out in faith, He would *restore the years the locust had eaten,* as Joel 2:25 says, and give me a future that was even more blessed and fulfilling than the season that had just ended.

I often write in my journals, and during that time I filled several journals with not only my thoughts and heart's cry but also the revelations from God's Word that He gave me daily while in

His presence. He literally breathed new purpose and new strategy for implementing my new season—and new courage to believe God that my latter would be greater than the previous.

Looking back on that experience, as much as I loved that season of my life, there's no way I would trade what I have experienced in the past fifteen years and honestly wouldn't want to go back if that were somehow possible. Now when I stand to minister in my own services, the anointing that I experience as I preach the Word of God and as I minister in the gifts of the Spirit is powerful and awesome. I literally can sense Him ministering through me, and I know that it would not have happened unless I had let Him turn my loss into a glorious recovery.

I had to let go of the past, as glorious and wonderful as it had been, and trust that what was coming would be even greater. I had the song "Moving Forward" in my car CD player and in my cell phone, and I played it over and over to get its message deep into my spirit. The following are some of the lyrics:

> I'm not going back, I'm moving ahead
> Here to declare to You my past is over in You
> All things are made new, surrendered my life to Christ
> I'm moving, moving forward.[4]

I wrote a note to Ricardo and thanked him for recording this song because the Holy Spirit literally breathed that message into my spirit and helped me to believe God for my future.

That brings me to the second way David brought about recovery. When you find the secret place of the Most High, true

4 Words and music by Israel Houghton, sung by Ricardo Sanchez, 2007.

worship begins to erupt from your spirit, releasing the peace of God and His abundance on your life.

Key 2: Encourage Yourself in the Lord by Praising God

David praised and worshipped the Lord! As stated earlier, David was a worshipper of the Most High God and had a long history of praising God, which is clearly expressed by the many psalms written by him. David knew that one of the most certain ways to recovery and restoration was to magnify God, despite the circumstance.

We see this in his conquest of the Philistine giant, Goliath, recorded in 1 Samuel 17. David's response to the taunting and threats of this foul-mouthed, belligerent bully is "classic David" when he says in 1 Samuel 17:45 (NIV): *"You come against me with sword and spear and javelin, but I come against you in the name of the Lord Almighty, the God of the armies of Israel, whom you have defied."* David had learned that it's sometimes not enough to speak to God about your problem—in this case the giant Goliath who was threatening him and the entire nation of Israel's very existence—you must speak to the problem (the giant) about your God! You must speak what the blood speaks about the situation!

What was David doing here? He was coming into agreement with what he knew about His God! He was magnifying or praising the Lord rather than the problem or giant that was standing in his way and threatening his very survival.

Praise puts everything into proper perspective!

David's focus was not on the problem, aka Goliath; his focus was on the Lord Almighty, evidenced by the last part of 1 Samuel 30:6. David had learned not to magnify the problem but rather to magnify the Lord. In so doing, the Lord gave him a divine strategy for defeating the enemy and for bringing about a victory. That's what praise will do! It becomes a mighty weapon in our hand, as Psalm 149:6 says, and paralyzes the giant or whatever threatens to destroy us, bringing it down.

Psalm 149:6 (NKJV) proclaims, *"Let the high praises of God be in their mouth, and a two-edged sword in their hand."* This verse tells us two specific things that praise does: 1) it strengthens our hand, the Word of God becomes a mighty weapon of warfare in our hands; 2) it paralyzes the enemy and stops him in his tracks!

When we praise the Lord, the Spirit of the Lord breathes hope and strength into us and makes the Word of God real and powerful in our hands. Then, in the power of the Spirit, we can use the Word, which is the sword of the Spirit, against the enemy to stop his attempts and bring restoration from the ashes of our lives. Praise is the beginning of our path to recovery. We encourage ourselves in the Lord when we come into agreement with what the blood of Jesus decrees over us and our lives.

I asked you earlier if you have experienced loss in the past. Another great story of how praise brought about recovery and restoration is found in the book of Ruth. Naomi, Ruth's mother-in-law, understood something of what you may have gone through. Not only did she and her husband, Elimelech, have to move to Moab because of famine (lack, shortage, loss), but soon after, her husband died. Ten years later, her two sons died. Now that's loss! But Ruth 1:7 gives us insight into what was the beginning of her recovery. Scripture says they returned to Judah. *Judah* means "praise." The path to recovery is praise. The beginning of our restoration is praise. Praise sets in motion heavenly intervention. Praise prepares the heart to receive. Praise softens our spirit to become receptive and submissive to the Word and will of the Lord, thereby setting us up for favor.

Key 3: Look for a Word from the Lord and Agree with God's Word

David looked for a Word from the Lord and agreed with the Word of God! This third key is found in 1 Samuel 30:7 (NKJV): "*And David said to Abiathar the priest, Ahimelech's son, 'Please bring the ephod here to me.' And Abiathar brought the ephod to David.*"

Abiathar was the priest, a man of God and a man of the Word. David asks him to bring the ephod, which was an apron-like garment that priests wore over their garment. From its earliest forms and uses, it appears that the ephod was associated with the presence of God or those who had a special relationship with God. It is portrayed as a source of divine guidance, as in this instance when David wanted to know if he should pursue the Amalekites (1 Samuel 30:7-8). David found the guidance he was looking for and decided to pursue or go after those who had caused him and his men such a tremendous loss.

When you are seeking to bring about recovery from a loss, it is vital to go to the Word of God and in His divine presence—let the Lord breathe hope, encouragement, wisdom, guidance, and divine strategy into your spirit that the blood decrees.

Key 4: Come Into Agreement with the Word—with What the Blood Decrees

However, it's not enough to just consult the Word; we must *come into agreement* with the Word for it to become a sword or weapon in our hands to take back what has been stolen and what is rightfully ours! We must come into agreement with what the blood speaks! This is why we must also surround ourselves with people who know the Word of God and will come into agreement in prayer with you to bring about your victory.

Sometimes our friends and even family members, as well-meaning as they may be, can hinder our faith if they are not in agreement with the Word of God. Jesus had to dismiss the mourners out of the room when he called for Lazarus to *"come forth,"* to be resurrected from the dead, because He knew their faith level was not where His was. Make sure that those you confide in are people of faith and people who will agree with you rather than bring you down or discourage your faith for recovery and restoration! Confide in people who know what the blood decrees!

KEY 5: ACT ON IT! GO AFTER WHAT BELONGS TO YOU! PURSUE LIKE DAVID DID!

If you read the story in 1 Samuel 30, you will see that in addition to the first three keys I have already given you, God gave David instruction to pursue the enemy: *"And He answered him, 'Pursue, for you shall surely overtake them and without fail recover all'"* (1 Samuel 30:8). What does that mean to us in our day? I believe it means go after the lost, whether it be a financial loss or a relationship loss or a spiritual loss. In the Spirit, we are to utilize the power that has been given us in His name, by His Word, through the weapons of warfare that are activated by the Holy Spirit. There may be nothing you can do in the natural realm; however, there's much that you can do in the spiritual realm. And when you do, the Lord will help you recapture stolen ground.

Let me share another situation in my life where we experienced a loss, but God miraculously brought about a recovery for my wife and me. You may recall the years from 2000 to about 2008 were years of economic growth and many were "flipping" houses and making a substantial profit in doing so. We bought a rental property in a thriving area of California about an hour from where we lived in Mission Viejo, California, at the time. We were advised that it could be quite profitable and seemed like a good investment.

For a while, all was going along well until our tenant decided not to pay the rent. After having promised month after month that he would pay, he eventually skipped town without paying what he owed us. To make matters worse, they left what was a charming brand-new house in horrible disrepair. Not only did we lose the rent money for six months but on top of that, we had to pay to remove the belongings they left behind, repair huge holes in the walls, paint the house, and more.

I have to be honest, I wasn't a "happy camper," as the expression goes. I wasn't angry at the Lord, and not so much angry even at these tenants who had taken advantage of us, but angry at the devil for robbing us. We amassed a debt of $10,000 in that six-month span related to the rental property, and I was very frustrated, to say the least! As mentioned earlier, sometimes you have to say to the devil, "Enough is enough!"

I have always been a person who tithes, not only giving 10 percent of my income (and then our income after we married), but in addition, we have given offerings above and beyond our tithes. I believe what the Word says about tithing! Our finances have always been blessed and although we weren't rich, the Lord had always blessed us with lovely houses, nice cars, and financial security for my family and me.

Now, suddenly, wham! We got hit with a tsunami of financial pressure because of this $10,000 unexpected debt! What did we do? We went to the Lord about it, just like David did in 1 Samuel, and started to believe God that we, like David, would *"recover all"!* Sometimes we Christians are too passive about what happens to us and the Lord wants us to do as David did—ask Him how to go after what is rightfully ours and take back what belongs to us. Take what the blood says is ours! This is exactly what I determined to do because I was angry that the devil had stolen from me—and in my spirit, I said, "Enough is enough!"

Shortly after that, I was ministering in a miracle crusade in Worcester, Massachusetts. During the morning service before the main speaker brought the message, another speaker was sharing some thoughts about giving before taking up the offering. Now I want to insert here that I have heard my share of preachers frankly manipulate people into giving a certain amount and make promises that in a week's time, they would receive a harvest, etc., and had been turned off by that as you have also probably been. I don't believe that gimmicks are ever appropriate when taking up an offering and quite frankly, I have seen enough that have sickened me and turned me off big time! That being said, I also realize that there is a divine principle involved in sowing seed into good ground and a blessing that can come to your life when you are obedient to the voice of the Lord when He lays it on your heart to give.

This particular morning, I listened with an open spirit and mind to the preacher and the Holy Spirit spoke to my heart to give an offering of $1,000. Now, $1,000 to me at the time was like $10,000 or more, and I honestly didn't even know how we would make it through the month financially because of an already strained budget. I remember going forward wondering, *Are you out of your mind, Jim?* But I knew that I had heard the Holy Spirit's voice, so I obeyed.

God is my witness—just one week later I received a call from a pastor's associate in Singapore asking me to come and lead worship for a conference that they were holding at their church. I tried to politely decline his offer due to my work obligations, but he was very persistent. He said, "We want to bless you, and we are paying for your entire trip." I felt in my spirit that I should accept and go to the conference.

I made the long trip and wouldn't you know, my luggage did not arrive with me when I landed in Singapore. It was only a few hours until the first service began, and I had no clothes to wear for the service except the ones on my back, certainly not appropriate for ministry. The host pastor's staff were most gracious and quickly took me to a shopping mall to buy a suit, shirt, shoes, etc., to wear that evening—and would not let me pay for the clothing. Favor!

The conference was great and after the last service, I headed to the airport to catch a red-eye flight back to California where we were living then. On my way out of the church, the associate pastor, who had initially contacted me about coming, handed me a thick white envelope and said, "My pastor wants you to have this." I was sort of surprised by it, but since I was in a hurry to get to the airport, I said, "Thank you very much," put the envelope in my briefcase, and left for the airport. Here's the restoration and recovery part of the story.

Several hours later, somewhere over the Pacific Ocean, I woke up from sleeping for a few hours and I heard the Spirit of the

Lord say to me, "Look inside the envelope." So, I pulled out my briefcase as quietly as possible, trying not to disturb the passengers around me. Then I turned on my light above my seat and opened the envelope. To my shock and amazement, I discovered the envelope contained $10,000 USD in crisp, new hundred-dollar bills! My heart was overjoyed when I realized that the Lord had not forgotten about our loss and had blessed my/our obedience in giving the $1,000, which I believe began a means of recovery for my wife and me after the tenant had left town without paying the rent they owed and left our house in shambles.

Divine Connections

In the case of David and his men going after the Amalekites who had robbed them, once God told him to pursue, God brought David a divine connection, a man who helped him locate the enemy. The man was an Egyptian slave of the Amalekites who had been left behind by his master because he was weak and sickly. In exchange for being an informant, telling David his enemy's location, David spared his life (1 Samuel 30:13-15).

As the story goes, because of this "divine intelligence," David and his men were led to the exact location where the enemy was and found them celebrating, eating and drinking with their defenses down. That night, David and his men overtook them and only 400 out of the thousands of Amalekite soldiers escaped—the rest were slain. Not only that, David and his men rescued their loved ones and took back *all* that had been stolen from them!

I believe that once we pray in the Spirit and come into agreement with what the blood decrees, the Spirit of God can breathe hope, divine strategy, and faith into our hearts for recovery by the Word of God. He will bring us divine connections, creative ideas and divine favor that will help us regain what we have lost, just like in our case after having been robbed by the enemy when my tenant failed to pay rent for months and destroyed our rental property.

God is in the business of recovery and restoration! His blood decrees recovery! After all, that's the whole reason He came to die for us in the first place! His blood shed on the Cross cried out "Restoration." Satan's plan to forever separate humankind from God was thwarted and a way was made to bring restoration and recovery of what was lost.

Some paint Him to be a God full of wrath just waiting to pounce on us if we mess up in the slightest but even here in the Old Testament, prior to the age of grace that we now live in, He showed Himself to be more than willing to forgive, to allow judgment to be averted, and to provide a path to restoration and abundance.

I don't know what loss you've experienced, my friend, or how it may have caused you tremendous emotional pain and despair. However, I do know that God wants to give you the testimony of David! He wants to bring beauty out of the ashes of your life, give you the oil of joy for mourning, and the garment of praise for the spirit of heaviness (Isaiah 61:1-3). I refer to this passage as "God's Divine Exchange Plan." Not a bad deal, aye?

While the Bible doesn't promise that all will be a bed of roses and that we as Christians will never experience hardship, trials, or tests of our faith, a recurring theme in both the Old and the New Testaments is that our God is the God of restoration and recovery.

However, often recovery is triggered and begins when we step out in faith to receive what has been paid for us by the blood. When we agree with the blood's decree!

Abraham obeyed God in leaving his country and going to a land that God would show him. That step of obedience began a process for God to restore his body to that of a young man who could father a child even at the ripe old age of 100, thereby enabling God to keep His promise of a son and to eventually make Abraham the father of multitudes.

The apostle Paul gave the church at Philippi a directive in Philippians 3:12 (NKJV): *"Not that I have already attained, or am already perfected; but I press on, that I may lay hold of that for which Christ Jesus has also laid hold of me."* He was telling them, and us today, to take what the Lord Jesus has already paid for and acquired for us. Lay hold of it; grasp it and don't let go of it. How do we do that? By hearing what the blood is decreeing, agreeing with it, and going after it in faith that the Lord will do it.

The blood of Jesus speaks recovery and restoration for your life today! I truly believe He will situate us for favor and for recovery from our losses if we will do as David did in 1 Samuel 30. Here's the end to that story about David and his men: *"And nothing of theirs was lacking, either small or great, sons or daughters, spoil or anything which they had taken from them; David recovered all"* (1 Samuel 30:19 NKJV).

Your testimony can be: "_______________ (insert your name) recovered all!"

DECREE

Today, by faith, I lay hold of what Christ has laid hold of for me. His blood speaks recovery and restoration for me, my family, my health, my finances, and all that pertains to me. I receive it by faith and ask for it in the mighty name of Jesus...because the blood says so!

TWELVE

The Blood Decrees Protection

We all have home insurance, auto insurance, health insurance, and so forth to protect in case of an accident, major disaster, or health event. The best insurance, however, is the *blessed assurance* of knowing you are covered by the blood of Jesus; it's comprehensive and there is no term limit and no deductible! The price has been pre-paid by the blood of Jesus on the Cross! The blood speaks protection!

While the children of Israel took their journey to the Promised Land, God miraculously protected them. Exodus 13:21 (NKJV) says, *"And the Lord went before them by day in a pillar of cloud to lead the way, and by night in a pillar of fire to give them light, so as to go by day and night."* If you know anything about that part of the world, which is mainly desert, during the day, the sun can be scorching and unbearable. The cloud not only was for their guidance but also provided a layer of protection from the harsh rays of the sun as they journeyed the long hours through the wilderness. The opposite extreme is also true in the desert; at night, the temperatures drop to almost freezing and so the pillar of fire provided warmth during the long, cold nights.

Exodus 14 describes the account of when the Egyptian army was pursuing the children of Israel. God instructs Moses to stretch out his hand holding the rod and the Red Sea divided so they could pass through unharmed and escape the enemy. Once they were safely on the other side, God instructed him once again to stretch out his arm with the rod and the waters closed over the Egyptians and they all drowned. At their darkest hour with nowhere to turn, God gave the Hebrews a miracle of divine protection and came through for them.

An interesting footnote to this biblical story: archaeologists have recently discovered the remains of the Egyptian army in the exact location of the sea where this mighty deliverance took place! Miriam, prophetess and Moses' sister, sang upon witnessing this amazing deliverance in Exodus 15:21, *"And Miriam answered them: 'Sing to the Lord, for He has triumphed gloriously! The horse and his rider He has thrown into the sea!'"*

Second Chronicles 20 gives us the account of when the Moabites and the Ammonites came against righteous Jehoshaphat, king of Judah (when the Israelites were divided into two factions). At first, like is often our reaction, Jehoshaphat fears because they were vastly outnumbered! After he receives the word of the Lord—the Word always brings courage and dispels fear—King Jehoshaphat rises in the strength of the Lord and God miraculously gives him a tremendous victory. The word he received from the Lord was. *"Do not be afraid nor dismayed because of this great multitude, for the battle is not yours, but God's"* (2 Chronicles 20:15 NKJV). On the strength of that word, the king instructs the singers to praise (praise will always bring about your victory), and God does something amazing because of their praise. The Lord *"set ambushes"* against the enemy and in their confusion, the armies kill one another, and God's people are divinely protected (2 Chronicles 20:22-23). No matter the size of the problem or enemy you are facing, it's no match for the protection of the blood of Jesus! The blood says so!

Throughout my life and especially over the past 40 years of ministry as I have traveled almost 4 million miles by air, in some very dangerous places on earth, I have relied on the promises in the Word of God for protection for not only me, but my family while I was away from them. He has blessed me with a shield of His protection, and I am grateful to Him for it. Some of those promises I share with you now.

Psalms and Promises

The Psalms are a tremendous reinforcement to the truth that God protects His own. The blood of Jesus decrees a shield of protection round about us.

Psalm 3:3 (NKJV) says, *"But You, O Lord, are a shield for me, my glory and the One who lifts up my head."* The presence of the Lord in our lives, or His glory, becomes a shield around us protecting us from danger and harm.

Psalm 23:4-5 (NKJV) says, *"Yea, though I walk through the valley of the shadow of death, I will fear no evil; for You are with me; Your rod and Your staff, they comfort me. You prepare a table before me in the presence of my enemies; You anoint my head with oil; My cup runs over."*

Psalm 34:7 (NKJV) tells us, *"The angel of the Lord encamps all around those who fear Him, and delivers them."*

One of my favorite psalms is Psalm 42:1: *"As the deer pants for the water brooks, so pants my soul after You, O God."* I've sung this psalm many times and led it in worship many, many times over the years of ministry.

Have you ever wondered why the deer pants for the water brooks? It's not just because it may be thirsty for a drink of water.

The deer knows instinctively that if it gets to the water, the predator pursuing it will lose its scent when submerged in the water. What a beautiful picture of the protection of the Lord provided for us as believers! Because of the presence of the Lord, represented by the water, we are divinely shielded and protected from the predator, the devil who according to the Word of God is as a roaring lion who seeks to devour us. Praise God we know that greater is God in us than the evil one that is in the world (1 John 4:4) The blood of Jesus purchased our protection. The blood decrees so!

As I elaborated in the chapter "The Blood Decrees Reconciliation" on our access to the presence of God, one of the most familiar and salient examples of God's protection in Scripture is the Passover and the prophetic instruction of God to Moses when He was about to free the people from the bondage of Egypt. They were instructed to take the blood of a lamb and put it on the doorposts of their homes. That blood speaking to the approaching death angel decreed, "This house is divinely protected! You have no power here! Access denied! No trespassing!" (See Exodus 12:22-23.)

That is, in fact, exactly what happened when they did as Moses instructed them to do. I can only imagine what those Israelites were thinking as they huddled in their homes, trusting in the word of Moses, that they would indeed be divinely shielded and protected from the existential threat of the enemy who was out to annihilate them. That blood on the doorposts of their homes spoke loudly, emphatically, and most importantly, prophetically!

The spiritual application for believers in Christ Jesus is unmistakably clear—the blood of Jesus covers our hearts and lives and is a divine shield protecting us from the attempts of the wicked one to harm us! So, how do we apply the blood today?

How to Apply the Blood of Jesus

We don't hear often enough teaching on how to apply the blood of Jesus. I thought it would be good to include this in this section because frankly, many do not know how to and suffer because of it. Also, you will see how it ties in closely with speaking what the blood speaks.

Revelation 12:11 (NKJV) is a verse most Christians are familiar with. However, do we realize that this verse contains three keys to how to overcome the devil?

> And they overcame him [satan] by the blood of the Lamb and by the word of their testimony; and the loved not their lives to the death.

Three things are mentioned in this verse: blood, word, and our testimony. For us to be overcomers, we must know what the blood decrees, we must believe the promises of the Word of God *and* declare them. Let the decrees come out of our mouths. However, there is something important to also remember in the last phrase of this familiar Scripture.

Frequently, people fail to quote the last phrase, *"and they loved not their lives to the death."* When you die to self and deny the flesh, the Holy Spirit is unhindered in supplying the power of the blood to bring breakthrough, or overcoming power. *"They loved not their lives"* means that they died to the dictates and desires of the flesh and self and were alive unto Christ. When you deny self and take up your cross and follow Jesus, the grace of the Lord purchased by His blood gives you access to all that is yours in Christ. Once you've surrendered your life to Christ, made Him the Lord of your life, then you can expect that the blood that speaks, the word of your testimony, will become effectual.

First, we must know *what* the blood entitles us to. We must know what it decrees! What it speaks over us! We learn that from the Word of God. Then, it is important to speak it! Let it come out of our mouths. When we do this, we disarm the devil and he is exposed by the truth. The Holy Spirit brings us revelation of truth and we can defeat the evil one.

Sometimes the only way to be delivered is to *speak* what the blood speaks over your traumatic circumstance and put the devil on notice that you know the One who has defeated him and that you agree with His Word. When we decree what the blood decrees, our spirits hear it as well and faith grows in our hearts.

If you are dealing with a bondage or addiction of any kind, hiding it won't help! Bring it out in the open to the Lord; He knows already and wants to hear that you're in agreement with what His blood decrees. Go to God and resist the devil by the blood and the word of your testimony. Speak it out to Him and make it personal. The word of your testimony of what the blood has done, what it has bought for you is powerful! He has redeemed you; you belong to Him! Satan and his demonic spirits have no power, no hold and no dominion over you. Let him know that! Speak it out of your mouth!

Psalm 107:2 says, *"Let the redeemed of the Lord say so!"* That phrase is not included in God's Word just for hyperbole! Something happens to your faith when you hear it come out of your mouth. The power of the blood is made real, made alive when you decree what it decrees! Have you ever noticed that when you testify or give a witness to someone, your own faith is made stronger? Speak what the blood has done for you! Speak what you believe it will do for your loved ones. Make it personal. It becomes effective when you do.

We are putting the devil on notice of what the blood has done for us and that's how we defeat him. He knows he's no match for the blood—but do we realize it? Speaking it reinforces it to our spirit and helps us to stand in it.

Today, many Christians are oppressed by demons because they don't know this. Knowing what the Word says about the blood, testifying about it, making it personal, and sharing what the blood has done for you gives you the power to overcome the devil and oppression.

Psalm 91:1-2 (NKJV) says, *"He who dwells in the secret place of the Most High shall abide under the shadow of the Almighty."* Amen! *"I will **say** of the Lord...."* Did you catch that? It's important to say it! Speak it. Decree it! Let the devil hear it come out of your mouth! Say what? *"...He is **my refuge, my fortress**, My God, in Him will I trust."* The devil doesn't want us to find that beautiful hiding place in the Lord! When we speak it, we find it.

We often fail to find deliverance because we are not speaking the promises that His blood speaks! Many would rather run to various "deliverance ministries," and there is a place for that. However, we ourselves, can bring about deliverance by speaking what the blood has done for us!

Often when someone else rebukes the devil on our behalf, if we don't know how to stand in that victory, we will most likely succumb to it again. Speaking what the blood says helps you stand, and the devil will realize he has no authority or power over you any longer.

Say: "I'm redeemed by the blood of the Lamb!" Put the devil on notice!

Second, or the second way to apply the blood is found in 1 John 1:7 (NKJV): *"If we walk in the light as He is in the light, we have fellowship with one another, and the blood of Jesus Christ His Son cleanses us from all sin."*

Confess that the blood cleanses you, say it. Declare, "I'm walking in the light, the blood cleanses me from all sin." That's how we resist evil and how we utilize the weapons of our warfare. (Psalm 107:2)

Say: "I'm walking in the light and the blood cleanses me; my sins are forgiven, and I am in fellowship with His body." Don't underestimate the power of fellowship that we have together in the body of Christ because of the blood. In the natural realm, family members share a bond that is different from what we share with friends or acquaintances. It comes because we are blood. Our mutual heritage because of blood binds us together.

I have cousins I don't see but maybe once or twice a year, but we maintain a closeness because we share the blood of our ancestors. How much more those of us in Christ share a bond that comes by His blood. It's amazing, but you can meet someone in the body of Christ and have only known them for a short while yet sense a bond that is strong and mutual in Christ. It comes because we are relatives through the blood of Jesus!

Third, Romans 5:8-9 (NKJV) tells us, *"But God demonstrates His own love toward us, in that while we were still sinners, Christ died for us. Much more then, having now been justified by His blood, we shall be saved from wrath through Him."*

Say: "I'm justified by the blood of Jesus. I'm delivered from wrath by the blood." Speak it out. Say so. Say: "I'm free, not guilty I'm justified." (Psalm 107:2)

Fourth, Hebrews 13:12-13 (NKJV) reveals, *"Therefore Jesus also, that He might sanctify the people with His own blood, suffered outside the gate. Therefore let us go forth to Him, outside the camp, bearing His reproach."*

"Go forth outside the camp" means share it! Tell it! We must declare it. I'm sanctified by the blood. I'm set apart by the blood and I'm free from satan's domain. I have access to God and the devil has no access to me. Only God has access to me. The devil can't even find me because I'm "hidden in Christ Jesus" because of the blood!

Set apart means to be transferred from the earthly kingdom to the heavenly Kingdom. We are not going to be sanctified—we are already sanctified by the blood.

Philippians 3:20 (NKJV): *"For our citizenship is in heaven, from which we also eagerly wait for the Savior, the Lord Jesus Christ."* We are already citizens in Heaven—satan has no access to us. Talk like it! Let your speech be indicative of the Kingdom of Heaven. Say it! "I'm a citizen of Heaven and no devils are allowed!"

Fifth, John 6:53-54 (NKJV): *"Then Jesus said to them, 'Most assuredly, I say to you, unless you eat the flesh of the Son of Man and drink His blood, you have no life in you. Whoever eats My flesh and drinks My blood has eternal life, and I will raise him up at the last day.'"*

The blood of Jesus has given us life eternal. We don't belong to the kingdom of death! We belong to the Kingdom of Life forever! We must declare it! Speak it out! Decree it!

Sixth, Hebrews 12:22-24 (NKJV): *"But you have come to Mount Zion and to the city of the living God, the heavenly Jerusalem, to an innumerable company of angels, to the general assembly and church of the firstborn who are registered in heaven, to God the Judge of all, to* *the spirits of just men made perfect, to Jesus the Mediator of the new covenant, and to the blood of sprinkling that speaks better things than that of Abel."*

If you think that applying the blood is for the Old Testament, right here in the New Testament in the book of Hebrews we see it. This passage says, we come *"to the blood of sprinkling."* That means we still must apply the blood. This is why so many are oppressed. No one has taught them to speak it! To apply the blood by speaking it. The Bible says speak it! Declare it! Decree it! When we do, the devil backs off.

Seventh, Hebrews 10:19-22 (NIV): *"Therefore, brothers and sisters, since we have confidence to enter the Most Holy Place by the blood of Jesus, by a new and living way opened for us through the curtain, that is, his body, and since we have a great priest over the house of God, let us draw near to God with a sincere heart and with the full assurance that faith brings, having our hearts sprinkled to cleanse us from a guilty conscience and having our bodies washed with pure water."*

"Let us hold fast the confession of our hope without wavering, for He who promised is faithful," (Hebrews 10:23 NKJV). Holding fast our *confession,* speaking it out in faith. This is what Hebrews 10:23 tells us to do.

Let's decree all seven of these ways to apply the blood while doing so:

DECREE

I've been redeemed by the blood.
I'm walking in the light by the blood.
I'm justified by the blood.
I'm sanctified by the blood.

> *I have life eternal by the blood.*
> *I have access to Jesus through the blood.*
> *I have access to the presence of God through the blood.*
> *I have access through His blood that is pleading and interceding for my case. Jesus is interceding for me; I cannot be defeated ever because Jesus is speaking on my behalf, pleading for me in Heaven.*

You may have heard the expression, "The devil can't cross the blood line." Once again, they are referring to the fact that the blood of Jesus is a holy barrier from satan's attempt to harm and destroy us. The phrase is derived from the example and story of the Passover, which we have discussed in detail; the blood on the door of your heart speaks, "No access" to the enemy. "No trespassing!"

Speaking what the blood decrees makes us aware that although the enemy may threaten and send his words to cause us to fear in our minds, we are protected by the blood.

When the Israelites applied the blood of the lamb, they applied it *in faith* that that blood would be a sign that this home was under the protection of Jehovah God!

Hyssop

One important thing to remember when applying the blood is this. It's one of the aspects that I love about how they were to apply the blood to their homes; they used hyssop to do it.

> Take a bunch of hyssop, dip it into the blood in the basin and put some of the blood on the top and on both

> sides of the doorframe. None of you shall go out of the door of your house until morning (Exodus 12:22 NIV).

Hyssop is a plant that grows prolifically in the Middle East. Hyssop has cleansing properties for the blood when digested. Besides the spiritual significance of it, it is interesting also to consider that digesting it has several health benefits.

I've been blessed to travel to Israel many times and to other countries in that region of the world. Because of that, I have eaten at various Middle Eastern restaurants. They will frequently serve bread made with *zaatar,* which as I understand it, is an herb made from hyssop.

Hyssop has powerful spiritual significance! It represents cleansing and faith! The blood of Jesus has been applied to our hearts, and it is good to remind ourselves of this fact. As referenced earlier, a common expression used in prayer in my home growing us was, "We apply the blood of Jesus." Or, "Cover them with Your blood, Jesus," my parents and grandparents would pray. What were they doing as they prayed those phrases? They were applying the blood and doing it in faith that the blood of Jesus would protect us, their children.

When we apply the blood of Jesus, we do it in faith that the blood decrees divine protection over us, our families, our homes and possessions, our future, and so on. Just as the blood spoke to the death angel, it speaks to the enemy of our souls, "This house belongs to the Lord!"

Remember, the apostle Paul reminded the Corinthians and us today through the Word of God in 1 Corinthians 3:16 (NKJV) when he asked the question, *"Do you not know that you are the temple of God and that the Spirit of the Lord dwells in you?"* We are the house of God today! Our homes, our houses are protected by the blood of Jesus! I still do the same for our family, my wife, son and daughter-in-law daily.

As a young minister working at what is now called Glad Tidings church in Bangor, Maine, when the holidays rolled around, I would sometimes make the nine-hour drive down to my home state of New Jersey to visit loved ones over the Christmas and New Year holidays.

On one trip it was snowing hard as I made my way down I-95 South toward New Jersey. I had been putting in a lot of hours for the Christmas production and was a little short on sleep, so I was having a hard time staying awake as the hours went by on the drive. I must have dozed off, and the next thing I knew, my car was careening down an exit ramp at 65 miles an hour about to plow into the cars that were stopped waiting for the light to turn green at the bottom of the ramp. Seconds before I was about to crash into them, I woke and slammed on the breaks—stopping just in time before what could have been a horrific accident. I have no doubt that the blood of Jesus protected me!

Another time, while working at a church in Trafford, Pennsylvania, once again the Lord spared my life. I had taken a position in San Jose, California, and had given my notice to the church in Trafford. Because I had to let go of my apartment, I was staying for a few days in a missionary apartment adjacent to the sanctuary of the church. After my going away party, somehow the door to the recreation center didn't close properly and the wind had blown it open.

The local police made it a habit to drive through the parking lot to check on the church. When they saw my car there in the early hours of the morning and the door open, they decided to enter to investigate. The inside door from the apartment opened directly into the sanctuary. I heard the office phone ringing and it woke me up. Because it wouldn't stop ringing, I decided I'd better go and answer it. The phone was in another wing of the building, so to get to it I had to open the door to a pitch dark sanctuary and make my way through the dark sanctuary to the light switch, then proceed to the where the phone was ringing.

The moment I opened the door to the sanctuary, a flashlight shined in my face, and I heard the words "Don't move!" Naturally I froze and through the reflection of his flashlight, I realized it was a police officer. I proclaimed with a stutter, "I, I, I'm one of the pastors here and I'm staying here temporarily." He reluctantly believed me and said, "I was about to shoot you." About then, all the adrenalin drained out of me, and I almost collapsed on the floor in a heap.

Once again, I know it was the protection of the blood of Jesus over me. *The fervent prayers of the righteous avails much* (see James 5:16). I'm grateful for parents who knew the power of the blood and what the blood speaks over us. The blood speaks protection!

My sister-in-law, Dorothy, tells a story of when she was a teenager growing up in a somewhat rough area of Boston. She happened upon some gang member girls. They circled around her with chains in their hands and were about to attack her. Knowing the power of the blood, she bowed her head and asked the Lord to cover her with His blood of protection. The leader of the group said, "For some reason I can't lay a hand on you," and they opened the circle and allowed Dorothy to walk right out. Speaking the blood of Jesus releases the power of the Lord's protection.

As mentioned previously, when researching the meaning of the word *Pesach,* the Hebrew word for *Passover,* the implication is that the Lord Himself hovered over the houses of the children of Israel protecting them. I love that! Now I know why back in my childhood, my grandparents and parents would often use the phrase in prayer, "Hover over them, Lord," when asking for protection for their grandchildren. They understood this truth so beautifully depicted in the story of the Passover. The Lord indeed hovers over us, protecting us, because His blood is on the door of our hearts. The blood says so!

As parents, Mindy and I have often prayed for the protection of the blood of Jesus over our son from the time he was a young child until this day.

The church we attended when our son, Daniel, was a child had an academy that met in an adjacent building to the sanctuary, where my office was. I was the minister of music at the church. After school, would be soccer practice and Daniel was part of the soccer team. They were the champs in the league that year!

One day, Mindy was waiting in the car line to pick up our son. She watched in horror as at the very moment Daniel went to cross the street, a young driver pulled speedily out of a parking place and hit him, sending him up into the air and onto the hood of the car. Then he slid off when the driver slammed on the brakes. Thankfully, he survived with only a few scratches, but it could have been a very different outcome to say the least! We knew that it was not just the soccer knee pads, elbow pads, and gear that protected him—it was the blood of Jesus that we had often spoken in prayer over him.

Just last year while Daniel and his wife were driving home from our house after a nice time together, a car unexpectedly pulled out in front of their car and there was no way to avoid crashing into it at 60 miles an hour. Seeing the photos of their car afterward made us wonder how anyone made it out alive. But once again, we praised our wonderful Jesus for His hand of protection on them and sparing their lives. The blood speaks protection!

When we speak the blood, apply it, hear its decree, we can know that the Lord's presence comes and He is protecting us from any of the devices or attacks of the enemy!

I find extremely interesting and overwhelmingly encouraging that the place where Jesus was crucified, Golgotha, is in the north. Why is that significant? Because Israel's enemies frequently came from the north. The north presented a constant existential threat to them geographically. In the providence of God, the Cross where Jesus was crucified and shed His precious blood was situated in the north; a symbolic block between us and the adversary of our souls, the devil.

Prophetically, it was pictured in the sacrifices of the Old Testament. Leviticus 1:11 (NKJV) tells us that they were instructed to sacrifice the animals on the north side of the altar: *"He shall kill it on the north side of the altar before the Lord; and the priests, Aaron's sons, shall sprinkle its blood all around on the altar."*

Hundreds of years before Jesus' blood would be shed, the priests were prophetically signaling that a perfect sacrifice would be made for humanity's sin and that His blood of sprinkling would speak victory and protection from the enemy of our souls.

God's protection is also seen in the well-known account found in Deuteronomy 2:1-3 (NKJV) when God tells the children of Israel to move north. Let's read it together:

> Then we turned and journeyed into the wilderness of the Way of the Red Sea, as the Lord spoke to me, and

> we skirted Mount Seir for many days. And the Lord spoke to me, saying: "You have skirted this mountain long enough; turn northward."

To give you some background here, they had been circling Mount Seir for some time and the word of the Lord comes to them basically telling them, "Enough! Move north!"

The name Seir, pronounced "say-eer" means "rough." How often when we experience rough patches in our walk with the Lord, our tendency is to get stuck there, failing to realize there's victory ahead of us.

As just described, north was not only the source from which their conflicts originated but also prophetically speaks of the victory won by Jesus. The blood of Jesus historically and especially today, stands between God's people and the enemy of God's people, the devil and his demonic forces.

How often we find ourselves "circling the mountain," stuck perhaps in a trauma or wound of the past, perhaps in a hurt caused by a betrayal by someone we trusted, perhaps caught in a spiral down of negative thoughts and oppression, unable to move ahead to what the Lord has for us today and for our future. Not to diminish in any way the trauma that many have faced; however, I believe the Holy Spirit allowed this account to be recorded in the Word of God, to remind us to move north toward the Cross. Allow the victory that Jesus' blood affords us to thrust us forward enabling us to take possession of all that His blood decrees is ours in Jesus' name.

Hebrews 12:1-2 tells us that even our Lord Jesus needed to focus on *"the joy that was set before Him,"* that being reinstated with the Father to sit at His right hand having finished the work that

He was sent to do, to endure. That is what helped Him endure the pain of rejection, the agony of the beatings and the excruciating suffering He endured upon that cruel Cross. We must follow His example, keeping our eyes fixed on the prize set before us and press on in faith *"toward the mark for the price of the high calling of God in Christ Jesus"* (Philippians 3:14 KJV). We can do this knowing that the blood of Jesus declares His divine enabling to do so.

In conjunction with this thought, it's important to remember that Jesus is referred to as *"the Alpha and Omega,"* Greek for the beginning and the end. In Aramaic and in Hebrew, the language that Jesus spoke, those letters are *aleph* and *tav*. *Aleph* means sacrificial ox (sacrifice) and He is before all things! *Tav* means the cross. What does that mean to us? It means that Jesus has the final say in all matters that concern us! His Cross and the blood cry victory for you and me in every facet of our beings and lives.

As much as we appreciate the knowledge and diagnosis of medical doctors, they do not have the final say! They may give us the best that their knowledge can afford, but the Great Physician, Jesus, His blood always has the final say! Our bank account or finances, may indicate shortage but the apostle Paul reminds us in Philippians 4:19 (NKJV), *"God will meet all your need according to His riches in glory by Christ Jesus."* When faced with what is seemingly an impossible challenge whether in our health, families, finances, or any aspect of our lives, let us remember that the blood of Jesus has the final say!

DECREE

Lord, today I come into agreement with what Your blood decrees over me. You are the *Aleph* and the *Tav;* You have the final say in all matters concerning me, my family, my health, my well-being. I accept the protection that Your blood speaks over me and my household. Today I move forward from any offense, trauma, hurt, or bondage that the wicked one meant to destroy me with. I move north in victory knowing that Your blood speaks protection over me. The blood says so!

THIRTEEN

The Blood Decrees Overcoming Power

We've already discussed previously the powerful verse, Revelation 12:11 (NKJV): *"And they overcame him by the blood of the Lamb and by the word of their testimony..."* and the powerful importance of coming into agreement with what the blood decrees. Let's look at another power-packed passage of Scripture recorded in the book of Ephesians, the apostle Paul's letter to the church at Ephesus, which was pastored by Timothy, his son in the gospel.

The apostle Paul told the church at Ephesus in his letter to them that the Lord has *"raised us up together and made us sit in heavenly places in Christ Jesus"* (Ephesians 2:6 NKJV). This was one of my first sermons I ever preached; and even back then, the revelation of this truth impacted me as a young man and minister.

Do we fully comprehend what this means? I often tell congregations that I'm preaching to these days the following, "You may be sitting here today, but that's not where you are seated! You're seated in heavenly places in Christ Jesus!" Jesus is seated at the right hand of the Father. That's a seat of power and authority. How amazing that we should be entitled to sit with Jesus in that seat because His blood paid the price for it and it decrees it. That's a seat far above principalities and powers and wickedness in high places. That's a placing where nothing can harm us. No demonic power has power over the blood of Jesus that is on our hearts. No plan or ploy of the devil can destroy a believer who knows what the blood decrees! We are more than conquerors.

All too often we allow ourselves to succumb to the lies of the devil that speak contrary to what the blood speaks. It's time to realize where we are seated in Christ and speak accordingly!

Using the example of the Passover again, the blood was a token on the homes of the children of Israel. You could say that it shouted at the death angel, "Don't mess with God's people! Don't even think about it! Get out of here! You have no power and no authority here." The blood that covers our hearts tells the same to the enemy today. He knows he's no match for the Lord! He knows his day is coming. Jesus' victory on the Cross delivered to us power and authority over the power of satan.

The events of the Lord's final week on earth before dying on the Cross and then resurrecting introduce us to a Greek word that has significant meaning. That word is *paradidomi,* which in Greek means "to surrender, to give into the hands of another" or to "hand over" to someone else.

As we read the account in the Gospels, we see that Jesus was first betrayed by Judas for 30 pieces of silver and "handed over" to the Sanhedrin; they in turn, "handed Him over" to Caiphas, the high priest where He was beaten and His face marred beyond recognition. Caiphas "handed Him over" to Pilate who washed his hands of the matter, had Jesus scourged, and then at the request of the mob, "handed Him over" to be crucified on the Cross.

Praise God that was *not* the last "hand over" though! After Jesus uttered those final words, "It is finished," and gave up the ghost and died, He descended into hell. The Bible tells us He stripped satan of his authority and power over us and demanded him to "hand over" the keys of death, hell, and the grave. Glory to God! Yet there was still one more "hand over." That happened when Jesus ascended out of hell and He "handed over" all authority and power of the wicked one to you and me! Luke 10:19 (NKJV) declares, *"Behold, I give you power to tread on serpents and scorpions, and over all the power of the enemy: and nothing shall by any means hurt you."* That's quite a handover!

Today, in the mighty name of Jesus and because the blood says so, we can tell the devil to "hand over" everything he has robbed from us!

Jesus says in John 10:10 (NIV), *"The thief comes to steal and kill and destroy; I have come that they may have life, and have it to the full."*

The enemy is a thief, and he wants to rob us of our peace, of our godly marriages, our children, our health, our finances, and more. We have the authority to tell him to "hand it over" because the blood decrees our authority to do so.

In Bible days, the areas surrounding the cities was where the shepherds in the fields would tend their sheep. Having been to Israel many times myself, I can attest to the fact that even to this day, you can see shepherds doing the same much like they did 2,000-plus years ago.

A common practice for the shepherds was to rub the sheep with olive oil, which was abundant because of the many olive trees there. Reason being, there are also an abundance of flies there that continually harass the sheep. The scent of the oil repels the flies and drives them away. In fact, the word *anoint* means "to rub or to smear."

In the spiritual sense, flies are symbolic of demons. When the oil of the anointing is rubbed on our lives, because of the blood of Jesus, demons are also driven away as they realize they are no match for the blood. The blood's presence on our lives says in effect, "Stay away. You have no authority here." What a blessed truth to know that in Him, in Christ, we are protected, and we have overcoming power because the blood decrees it so!

Ephesians 6 gives us a holy arsenal of weaponry that we can employ by the power of the Holy Spirit against any attack of the enemy. The blood of Jesus on our hearts entitles us access to them. That blood decrees the title deed to them for our use.

The apostle Paul instructs us in 2 Corinthians 10:4-5 (KJV) that:

> (For the weapons of our warfare are not carnal, but mighty through God to the pulling down of strong holds;) casting down imaginations, and every high thing that exalts itself against the knowledge of God, and bringing into captivity every thought to the obedience of Christ.

So, how do we do that? We do that by believing in the authority that Christ's blood decrees that has been handed over to us. By not allowing our minds to be controlled, manipulated, or deceived by the lies, destructive thoughts that the enemy brings to challenge the authority of the knowledge of God. Rather to meditate on and speak or decree what the blood of Jesus has spoken and still speaks over us!

One day as I was reading 2 Corinthians 10:4, *"the weapons of **our** warfare,"* the word *our* seemed to jump out at me from off the page. I believe I was given a revelation about what the apostle Paul was trying to convey to the believers in Corinth. When he uses the word *our,* he most likely was not only using it in the corporate sense, as in the body of Christ.

Looking at the whole of his writings about our partnership with the Holy Spirit—such as in Romans 8:26 where he says, *"Likewise the Spirit also* ***helps*** *in our weaknesses,"* we become aware that the *our* he is talking about is you and the Holy Spirit. That combined partnership utilizing the weapons the Spirit, empowers us to use, *"is mighty through God to the pulling down of strongholds."* As believers, we are in partnership with the Spirit of the Lord, provided by the blood of Jesus, and have at our disposal the ability to cooperate with the Holy Spirit to bring down strongholds and attempts of the wicked one to defeat us.

DECREE

Today, because of Jesus' death and resurrection, I now have His Spirit living in me. I am seated in heavenly places with Christ Jesus far above all principalities and powers—and no weapon formed against me shall prosper, and every tongue that rises against me in judgment You, Lord, shall condemn. I remind the devil of his impending doom and that he has been defeated by the blood of Jesus! This is my confession according to Isaiah 54:17.

Today, I accept my partnership with the Holy Spirit and I "take hold together" against the stronghold that seeks to destroy me and my household (Romans 8:26). I am *"more than a conqueror"* (Romans 8:37) and no plans, schemes, or devices of the enemy will prosper against me. I overcome by the blood of the Lamb and by the Word of my testimony (Revelation 12:11)—because the blood says so!

FOURTEEN

THE BLOOD DECREES FAITH

Hebrews 11:1 (NKJV) tells us, *"Faith is the substance of things hoped for, the evidence of things not seen."* I particularly like to read this verse in the Amplified Version, Classic Edition:

> Now faith is the assurance (the confirmation, the title deed) of the things [we] hope for, being the proof of things, [we] do not see and the conviction of their reality [faith perceiving as real fact what is not revealed to the senses].

As part of our inheritance as "the children of Abraham," we have received the same faith that caused him to believe and receive the promise God had made to him without wavering. Romans 4:20-21 (KJV) tells us, *"He staggered not at the promise of God through unbelief; but was strong in faith, giving glory to God; and being fully persuaded that, what he had promised, he was able also to perform."*

As part of our inheritance in Christ, because of what His blood decrees, we too, are the recipients of this kind of unwavering faith that transferred to us through the blood of Jesus, His death on the Cross.

"How do you know that?" you ask. Good question! The answer, the Bible tells me so in Galatians 3:7 (KJV): *"Know ye therefore that they which are of faith, the same are the children of Abraham."* Faith in what? Faith in Christ Jesus and His work on the Cross for us. As Abraham's children, faith is part of the birthright passed down to us. The blood of Christ transferred that blessing to us.

This kind of faith is the assurance, the confirmation and title deed of things we hope for when we pray and believe what the blood decrees. The Amplified Bible, Classic Edition of Hebrews 11:1 says, *"faith perceiving as real fact what is not revealed to the senses."* In other words, just because you can't see it with your natural eyes, doesn't mean that it doesn't exist in the heavenly realm. This was the case with Abraham of old.

Romans 4:17 (KJV) tells us that Abraham believed *"...even God, who quickeneth* [makes alive] *the dead, and calleth those things which be not as though they were."* God does not see from our limited, finite perspective. He calls into existence in the heavenly realm things that may not be visible in the natural realm. This is the realm where faith operates. Scripture tells us that God has given to every person a measure of faith. When we speak what the blood decrees, I believe that measure is increased, and things are set in motion in the heavenlies that will eventually appear or manifest in the earthly.

Mountain-Moving, Giant-Slaying Faith

If you are facing a seemingly impossible situation today, I urge you to ask the Lord to impart to you this kind of mountain-moving, giant-slaying believing that even if you don't see it yet, you will. An Ephesians 3:20 (NKJV) kind of faith that believes what the apostle Paul wrote about our God, *"Now to Him who is able to do exceedingly abundantly above all we can ask or think...."*

I also encourage you to ask for *the gift of faith* to operate in your life and circumstance. What is the gift of faith? It is one of the nine gifts listed in 1 Corinthians 12 that are the gifts, or operations, of the Holy Spirit in the church. You mean you can ask for them? Absolutely! The apostle Paul says in 1 Corinthians 12:1 (NIV), *"Now about the gifts of the Spirit, brothers and sisters, I do not want you to be uninformed* [ignorant]."

Sadly, many in the church, even if they are not ignorant (unaware) of the gifts, they haven't been taught to expect them to operate in their life or to ask for them to do so. Would the Holy Spirit have inspired them to be recorded in Holy Writ if they weren't available to the church today? I think not! When this happens to you, or should I say *in* you, a supernatural deposit of faith is imparted in you to believe. It's a knowing that even transcends your thought processes that it's going to happen—even when there's no visible reason to believe it will. Some things you just know by the witness of the Spirit in you. This is how the gift of faith operates.

Let me share a testimony with you that is an example of how this gift can operate for us.

Prior to moving to Texas in 2011, I was in my study in our home in California meditating and praying over several of our needs. It happened to be a season when we were in a large amount of debt with two mortgages totaling over $600,000 plus credit card debt, student loan debt for our son's college education—and we struggling financially under the load of it.

For years I had been on staff of a major ministry, and by the time I left in early 2010, we had been making a comfortable salary. Now, having entered a new season of ministry by the leading of the Holy Spirit, suddenly the rug was pulled out from under us financially, so to speak, and our income was dependent on "love gifts" from churches where I ministered. Although I am so grateful for how the Lord miraculously sustained and supplied us, it wasn't enough to keep up with the load on us financially.

Ask Me, Believe Me

Back to my praying about it in my study…

One particular day I heard what I believe was the Lord speaking to me in my spirit, "Why don't you ask for the gift of faith or a word of faith concerning this debt? Why don't you believe Me for a mortgage-free home?" These words jarred me for a few moments and my mind began to race thinking about what I heard.

At first I began to think thoughts such as, *This can't or doesn't happen to guys like me, does it?* I had heard ministers with large followings testify how God had supernaturally paid off their ministry's debts or their homes, but did God really want me to believe that He would do it for us? I felt the gentle but real rebuke from the Lord saying to me, "I show no favoritism, Jim. Because I did it for them, I can do it for you too!"

Suddenly, faith was birthed in my heart to believe God for it. I got out my journal and wrote it down immediately. The prophet Habakkuk said, *"Write the vision and make it plain"* (Habakkuk 2:2 NKJV), and I have always believed that when God speaks something to your heart, it's a good idea to write it down. I believe writing it down quickens your faith and even sets things in motion supernaturally.

Long story made short, for a while I held on to this and it was very real to me, believing God would do it. After about six months though, I had forgotten about it to be honest.

One day, still under the pressure of the large debt we were carrying, my wife and I simultaneously said to each other, "Texas." I, we, had never thought about moving to Texas; and to be honest, I did not want to leave the beautiful area of southern California where we lived. However, our only son had married a sweet girl from Texas and they decided to make Texas their home. This made moving more appealing as we didn't like the prospect of living so far away from them.

We made the decision, put our house up for sale, and it sold very quickly. Before we knew it, we were making the drive from California to Texas. Now began our search for a house in the Hill Country of Texas. We found a house we liked and applied for a mortgage (forgetting about the word of faith I had received months earlier). Wouldn't you know, we got turned down. This was a first for us as our credit had always been very good and we never before had any problem obtaining a loan of any kind. However, since we had not been receiving a regular payment with paystubs to verify our income that we were able to make the monthly loan payments, the bank thought we were too much of risk and understandably so.

At first we were discouraged thinking, *What are we going to do?* Then, as I was in prayer one day I heard these words in my spirit, "Weren't you believing Me for a mortgage-free home?" I said, "Yes, Lord, thank You for reminding me!" I dug out my journal where I had written it down and once again faith began to swell in our hearts to believe God for it.

Shortly after this, the thought "happened" to come to my mind, *I wonder if we could take a loan from our annuity to pay the amount needed to secure a loan?* I called and asked about it and the agent said, "As a matter of fact, there is a one-time provision for you to take a loan out," and then gave the terms for repayment and how to apply for it. I hurriedly completed the paperwork and submitted the application, and within a matter of days we received the check for the necessary amount. That, coupled with the equity we had from our home sale in California, was enough to purchase another home that we found in that same area.

I will never forget the clerk's response when we put the offer in on the home and signed the docs to purchase it. She asked, '"Now how will you be financing the home, Reverend Cernero?" Excitedly I replied, "We're not! We are paying for it in cash." She was a bit taken back by my response at first but then quickly replied, "Well, that's great."

After a few short months, miraculously we had completely paid off that loan from my annuity and so now there we were, for the first time in our married life, the owners of a beautiful home with *no mortgage!* For all the years previously when I had been making a comfortable salary, we had never owned our homes outright; we always had large mortgage balances and large monthly payment amounts. I truly believe that what the Lord spoke to me was the *gift of faith* in operation for us.

I share this not in any way to brag, but to rather boast in the Lord! It was an Ephesians 3:20 moment in our lives! Because He did it for us, He can do it for you as well. Why not believe God for a *word of faith* and for this gift of faith to operate for whatever it is you have been praying for and believing God for in your personal life, your business, or your ministry? The blood of Jesus speaks *better things* for us, and faith to believe God for the impossible is included in those *better things!*

Since then we have moved twice, for different reasons, and in each case we still have no mortgage even though these were much newer homes.

I hesitated to share this story at first because of my potentially being classified as a "prosperity gospel" preacher, but then I thought again. As I stated in "The Blood Decrees a Seat at the King's Table"chapter, I realize there has been much unbiblical teaching about giving and there has been definitely gimmickry used by some to manipulate God's people. (Believe me, I've seen it all and have been grieved in my spirit over it!) We mustn't negate the truth of the Word of God. He's the One whose Word says that He will *"supply all your need according to His riches in glory by Christ Jesus"* (Philippians 4:19 NKJV).

The Lord knew that we had given our lives to ministry and that in order to fulfill that call, we needed to come out from under the strain and bondage of debt—and He took care of it! Praise God! I do believe though, it was when Mindy and I embraced the word of God in faith and the gift of faith, which was birthed in my spirit and in operation in our hearts, that the miracle of provision was initiated by the Lord. I encourage you to do the same.

If you are struggling in your faith, remember that the Word of God says, *"faith comes by hearing and hearing by the Word of God"* (Romans 10:17 NKJV). The more the Word of God is made *rhema* to us—made real to us by the Holy Spirit—faith comes to our hearts. It's our inheritance in Christ because the blood of Jesus says so!

The apostle John recorded this salient verse about faith in 1 John 5:4 (NKJV). *"For whatever is born of God overcomes the world. And this is the victory that has overcome the world—our faith."*

If you've been born again, *"born of God"* as 1 John 5:4 says, His blood declares that you are the recipient of this overcoming faith in Christ Jesus; faith that overcomes the world. Faith that overcomes, period!

DECREE

Today I hear this *better thing* that the blood of Jesus speaks over me—faith. Unwavering faith like Father Abraham and faith that overcomes the world (1 John 5:4). I have the *substance of things hoped for, the evidence, and the proof of things not seen,* and I stand on this promise that the Word of God has spoken to me, because the blood says so!

FIFTEEN

The Blood Decrees the Blessing of Abraham

Christ purchased our freedom and redeemed us from the curse of the Law and its condemnation by becoming a curse for us—for it is written, "Cursed is everyone who hangs [crucified] on a tree (cross)"—in order that in Christ Jesus the ***blessing of Abraham*** *might also come to the Gentiles, so that we would all receive [the realization of] the promise of the [Holy] Spirit through faith*

(Galatians 3:13-14 AMP).

Did you know that the blood of Jesus decrees that we are inheritors of the blessing of Abraham?

Genesis chapters 1 through 12 give us the story of the patriarch Abraham—how God called him to leave his family and his country and promised him that he would become a father of nations. God's covenant of blessing with Abraham was an eternal covenant; it will never end.

Imagine that you are this man, who was originally named Abram, and one day you're just going along par for the course, and suddenly you have a supernatural visitation from none other than the Lord God Himself. That alone would be enough excitement and a life-altering experience—but on top of that, He (God) speaks and says something amazing to you that your mind cannot even begin to conceive is possible because up until now, there is no evidence in your life to even give you a glimmer of hope that it will happen!

Here's what God said to Abraham:

> Now the Lord had said to Abram: "Get out of your country, from your family and from your father's house, to a land that I will show you. I will make you a great nation; I will bless you and make your name great; and you shall be a blessing. I will bless those who bless you, and I will curse him who curses you; and in you all the families of the earth shall be blessed" (Genesis 12:1-3 NKJV).

As amazing as this encounter with the Most High God was, what's even more amazing is that Abram believed what God told him and immediately obeyed God and did exactly what He said. He picked up his belongings and left his home, his extended family, his livelihood, and his country and set out to find the land that God had spoken to him about.

"So Abram departed, as the Lord had spoken unto him; and Lot went with him: and Abram was seventy and five years old when he departed out of Haran" (Genesis 12:4 KJV). Now that's faith! That act of faith was the key that began to unlock the blessing in his life and changed his destiny forever! Often an act of faith, a stepping out of your comfort zone and taking a risk is necessary for us to open the door to blessing and begin to realize God's abundant provision and promise.

I'm sure that Abram's family back in Haran must have thought he had lost his mind, probably saying, "You're going to do what,

Abram? Leave your familiar surroundings, your country, your family, your religion, and go to a strange land that you know absolutely nothing about? You must have been in the sun a little too long, son!" However, Abraham, according to Romans 4:17 (NKJV), *"believed God who…calls* [speaks into being] *those things which do not exist as though they did."*

Abram was 75 years old when God spoke to him and when he left his country in obedience to the divine directive he received. Now fast-forward to when Abram is 99 years old (Genesis 17:1) and after 24 years of holding on to the promise that God made him and to the Word of the Lord, he has yet to experience the fulfillment of the promise. However, God appeared to him again and assured him He hadn't forgotten His promise.

> And when Abram was ninety years old and nine, the Lord appeared to Abram, and said unto him, I am the Almighty God; walk before me, and be thou perfect. And I will make my covenant between me and thee, and will multiply thee exceedingly (Genesis 17:1-2 KJV).

At the end of verse 1, the Lord says to Abram, *"walk before me, and be thou perfect."* When we encounter the Spirit of the Lord, the Almighty, we begin to walk in new territory. In this enlarged territory, He perfects or makes whole every dimension of our lives—body, mind, soul, and spirit. It is a realm of fullness that cannot be attained by any other means but by Him pouring Himself into us. And just as a branch receives its life and sustenance from the vine, so we receive divine life from Him. This word *perfect* not only means blameless but also complete or whole.

COMPLETE TRUST

Very often God will allow us to come to the end of ourselves, our ability, and our resources so that the only thing we can do is to completely trust Him and lean on Him to bring about a supernatural miracle of divine supply and enabling.

You will notice in Genesis 17:1 that when Abram again has an encounter with the Lord, the El Shaddai, he is 99 years old and completely beyond the age reproductively to father a child. Suddenly, the finite meets the Infinite One, the deadness of his body in its ability to reproduce meets the Living God, the Giver of Life; the earthly meets the heavenly One; the natural meets the Supernatural and when that happened, Abram was suddenly connected to the miraculous, healing, creative power of the Almighty.

In fact, His name *El Shaddai* is derived from the Hebrew word *shad,* or breast. It is the connotation of a mother bringing her completely dependent child to her breast to satisfy the hunger and provide the nourishment needed for life to be sustained. The child would die apart from the nourishment from the mother and is totally dependent on her for life. So it was with the patriarch Abraham; prior to this life-altering visitation of the Most High, he was unable to produce a child. The moment he encountered divine supply, the El Shaddai quickened his body and supplied what only He could give, life. He is the Spirit of life.

In this amazing encounter with the Almighty, God reiterated His covenant of blessing that He made with Abram and changed his name from Abram, exalted father, to Abraham, father of many nations.

> And Abram fell on his face: and God talked with him, saying, As for me, behold, my covenant is with thee, and

> thou shalt be a father of many nations. Neither shall thy name any more be called Abram, but thy name shall be Abraham; for a father of many nations have I made thee. And I will make thee exceeding fruitful, and I will make nations of thee, and kings shall come out of thee. And I will establish my covenant between me and thee and thy seed after thee in their generations for an everlasting covenant, to be a God unto thee, and to thy seed after thee (Genesis 17:3-7 KJV).

Today, very often we choose a name for a baby that's about to be born because we like the name or the way the name sounds coupled with another name and surname, but not so in biblical times. Names were very important. To have a name that didn't truly represent you was a problem. For example, it might have been a little embarrassing for Abram to be called "exalted father"—because in reality he had no biological offspring!

But when God is about to do something extraordinary through you or in you, He will often "call" you, or "re-name" you according to how He sees you, not how others, as well-meaning as they may be, see you or perceive you. Your parents, as much as they may have loved you and desired the very best for you, might not have imagined what God has put in you. You might not even be aware of what potential is locked deep inside of you just waiting to be released. You may not recognize what talents God has placed in you that at present are lying dormant, but *He* knows! He put them there in the first place and called them over your life long before you were born.

You may not yet comprehend the full scope of what God wants to do through you and bring about in your life, but He does! A moment in His presence like Abram had and your eyes will open, and you will discover His plan for your life and just how much He wants to bless you!

Miraculous grace was dispersed into Abram's body, so much so that it necessitated a name change as his very disposition and destiny were forever altered in that divine moment.

The Big Deal

As referred to already, originally Abraham and Sarah's names were Abram and Sarai. These were their given names "before" God significantly and supernaturally blessed them and changed them in Genesis 17:5. You might be wondering, *So what? What's the significance of their name change? What's the big deal?* The answer: it's a VERY big deal, and when you understand, I believe you will agree! Let me explain why that is the case.

Something extraordinary happened because of the encounter Abraham had with El Shaddai in Genesis 17. Not only did the Lord reiterate His promise to him—the promise that he would have a son and that he would be the father of many nations—but He also changed his name. It is interesting to me that this is recorded in Genesis 17:5. You will understand why I said that in a few minutes as I continue to unpack this truth for you.

You see, there are no meaningless details in the Word of God, and if we will ask the Holy Spirit to reveal truth to us, He will open the hidden treasures. In fact, right now, while you're reading this chapter, why not stop for a moment and ask the Holy Spirit to "open the eyes of your understanding" and reveal this truth to you? I promise you, if you do, He will do it for you.

Before I comment on the first part of this amazing declaration the Lord makes over Abram, let me draw your attention to the wording of the last phrase of Genesis 17:5, *"for a father of nations* ***have*** *I made thee."* Notice the tense here, *have.* In other words, it had already been accomplished. God didn't say I am *about to* make you, or I *will eventually* make you. No. The Hebrew word here translates to the English past tense, *have.* This is because it exists outside of time as we know it! When God speaks or calls things, He calls it the way He sees it or the way that it is in Heaven. When our faith is quickened or made alive like Abram's was, we enter that timeless realm where God exists—and miracles happen!

When the Lord speaks a promise over us, He speaks in a tense that is most true and accurate; He speaks as though it has already happened or been accomplished, because it has! In Matthew 12:13 (and Luke 6:10) when Jesus, the Son of God, walked the earth hundreds of years after Abraham did, He met a man with a crippled arm. In response to this man's need, Jesus didn't say to him, "I see your hand is crippled," or "withered," as the King James version puts it. He didn't state what was obvious in the natural. No, He called it the way He saw it. He said to the man, *"Stretch out your hand."* Why? Because that's the way He saw it—fully functioning and perfectly whole. That's why He could ask the man to do something that in the natural seemed ridiculous. When we begin to see things the way Jesus sees them as already done and begin to call or speak according to what His Word says, we will see faith manifested in our lives and situations.

Now, let's turn our attention to the name change that is recorded in the first part of Genesis 17:5 (KJV). The Lord tells Abram, *"Neither shall thy name anymore be called Abram, but thy name shall be called Abraham; for a father of nations have I made thee."* As I said earlier, hidden inside this amazing account is a powerful, transformative truth.

TRANSFORMATIVE TRUTH

I have been a Christian all my life and I was brought up in a Spirit-filled home and church, attended Bible college, and heard countless sermons, but in all my years of Christian life, I must admit, I didn't truly understand this truth until about two decades ago. While studying Genesis 17, the Holy Spirit opened my understanding of this revelation. It has not only impacted my life in a dynamic and awesome way, but it has done so also to those with whom I have shared this message over the past years as I have preached this truth.

The blood decrees to us the Blessing of Abraham; truly this transformative truth can revolutionize your life in a powerful way.

There's a very powerful revelation here! You see, there's a significant difference between the Hebrew alphabet and the English alphabet, and most other languages for that matter. The letters of the English alphabet are just letters with no meaning or significance. Letters make words; words put together convey a thought, and so on. That is not the case in the Hebrew language. Every letter of the Hebrew alphabet is a word with a meaning and has a corresponding picture. For an example, if you look at Psalm 119, the longest psalm in the Bible, in most translations you will see that it is divided into sections and above those sections, are the letters of the Hebrew alphabet: *aleph*, meaning beginning, first or sacrificial lamb; *bet or beth*, meaning house; and so on.

If you travel to Israel, as you drive down the highways and roads, you will see street signs such as "Beth-shan" or "Beth-lehem," meaning Beth or house of whoever's name follows it. This is where we get the word *Beth-El* or house of God.

Amazingly, when you come to the fifth letter of the Hebrew alphabet, it is the letter *He* or *Hey* and sometimes spelled *Hei.*

Again, I believe it is significant that it is the fifth letter as five is the number of grace in the Bible. Grace is exactly what the patriarch Abram received, and it is captured in the new name given to him by the Lord.

To us, it just looks like an "h" was inserted into his name, but what was imparted was far greater than just a consonant. This letter and word "He" or "Hey" means the Spirit of the Lord. He is the Spirit of Grace, the significance being that apart from the supernatural impartation that Abram received, he would never have received the fulfillment of the promise that he would be the father of many nations or even one son, for that matter. Even more interesting and more revealing is the way this letter is pronounced. It is not articulated with the lips or the tongue but rather sounds like an exhalation of breath.

When I preach this message, I breathe forcefully into the microphone to further drive home this truth, but I believe you can grasp this awesome truth without the sound effects. Here's the mighty truth contained in this verse. When God inserted the "Hey" or His Spirit into Abram's name and body, He breathed or exhaled His life-giving, healing, restoring, renewing, creative, and quickening power into the deadness of Abram's body, making his body like that of a 24-year-old young man who now could father a child. Now, the miracle could take place! Anything that God breathes into comes alive! That is exactly what happened to this 99-year-old man.

Abram's body was transformed by the power of the Holy Spirit, symbolized in the name change given to him. From that moment on, he was no longer Abram but Abra-ham for the breath of the Spirit was now in him. In that glorious moment, he was translated to a new realm of faith and possibility—an enlarged territory. In this place, or territory, the miraculous power of the Spirit of the Lord operates.

BREATH OF LIFE

It is not unlike what happened to Adam in the Garden of Eden. Adam would have remained a lump of clay if the Lord hadn't breathed into his nostrils, and when He did, Adam became a living soul at that very moment. Romans 8:11 (paraphrased) tells us, *"...the Spirit of Him who raised Christ from the dead dwells in you, and He will quicken [breathe life or make alive, renew, restore, heal] your mortal bodies!"* Yes, the very same Holy Spirit who raised Christ from the dead in resurrection power is living and breathing in you and me, bringing us life and life more abundant.

God not only performed this amazing miracle in Abraham's body but also in his wife's body. You will recall that prior to this infilling of the Spirit and impartation of miraculous power, her name was Sarai. When God breathed the *hey,* or His Spirit's life-giving, restorative breath into her body, He changed her name to Sar-ah. Suddenly, this old woman's womb became like the womb of a 24-year-old woman who could produce an egg, be fertilized and bring to full gestation a perfectly whole male child—not just any child but the son of promise, Isaac.

Let that truth sink into your spiritual consciousness and heart. Whatever He, the Spirit of the Lord, breathes on or into, receives life, health, power, strength, renewal, and quickening. Perhaps your health has declined and the doctor's report isn't very encouraging. Perhaps your marriage is strained and the love that was once there seems to have died, and all that's left is going through the motions, or its even further decayed to the point that the word *divorce* has now been uttered. Worse yet, you feel dead in your spirit, and you feel far from the Lord, and the intimate fellowship and relationship you once shared with Him now seems a distant memory. Maybe your child, who you raised up in the house of the Lord, wants nothing to do with Him or the things of God.

Don't give up, my friend, if you find yourself experiencing and relating to any of these situations or other areas of your life that seem dead, nonproductive, or hopeless; realize this powerful truth for you today! There is nothing that you are going through that the breath of the Holy Spirit cannot change and transform! The blood decrees it! I have experienced it in my life on many occasions and seen situations that once seemed insurmountable and impossible change, and what was once dead come back to life. Because He did it for me, He can and will do it for you!

His Presence

Let me remind you, though, it was in the presence of the Almighty, the Lord, God Jehovah-Rapha (the Lord who heals) that quickened and transformed Abraham both spiritually and physically! In His presence is where we receive power—resurrection power (Romans 8:11) that heals, delivers, restores, renews, and brings back life to the dead areas of our lives. The blood decrees it! The blood says so!

God honored Abram's step of faith and his ability to believe in God's promise, and that set into motion a wave of favor, miracles, and blessings that his descendants are still benefiting from today!

I have witnessed powerful miraculous demonstrations in my life and the lives of those I've ministered to when there was a revelation of this truth—what the blood decrees is ours as inheritors of the Blessing of Abraham. Through the blood of Jesus on the Cross, the promised blessing was transferred to us! (See Galatians 3:13-14.)

Perhaps after reading all of this you still question in your heart, *Is this really for me? After all Jim, I'm not a Jew by ethnicity; I'm a Christian. How do you know that this truth about the Blessing of Abraham applies to me or to Christians in general? Besides, isn't that essentially an Old Testament message? Aren't we New Testament believers? Are we entitled to this blessing? If so, how do we as believers today use it?*

I mentioned it earlier but let me remind you here that this blessing is definitely our inheritance as the children of Abraham. Galatians 3:6-7 (NKJV) says, *"Just as Abraham 'believed God, and it was accounted to him for righteousness.' Therefore know that only those who are of faith are sons of Abraham."*

Let me ask you this question one more time: Are you of faith? By that I mean, have you believed on the Lord Jesus Christ, acknowledged your need of forgiveness from sin and accepted Him as your Savior? If yes, then the fact is, the Bible says you are *of faith* and you are a child, a son or daughter, of Abraham. Those who have believed on Him and accepted Him by faith are part of the body of Christ. If you have answered this ultimate question and accepted Jesus Christ as your Lord and Savior, then as a son or daughter of Abraham, the blessing of Abraham belongs to you too!

This is the first and most important step to receiving the blessing of Abraham in your life.

If you cannot honestly answer this question, I have very good news for you as well. Salvation and righteousness, the act of getting saved or salvation, is quite simple—it comes down to believing and confessing!

If you will pray the following prayer with me now, I can assure you that after you do, you will be saved and you will be able to say and agree with the apostle Paul that you are of faith and qualify for the blessing that the blood decrees over you.

Prayer

> *Lord Jesus, I believe You are the Son of the Living God. I believe You came and died for my sins on the Cross of Calvary. That Your shed blood decrees redemption, salvation, and infilling of Your Holy Spirit in my heart. I ask You to forgive my sins and cleanse my heart. Make me a new creation in Your Son, Christ Jesus. Help me to live for You from this day on. I now confess You are my Lord, my Savior, and I thank You that according to Your Word, I am saved. Amen!*

If you just prayed that prayer with all your heart, you are now a Christian and are saved. You are also "of faith" according to the Word of God, a child of Abraham. That means all that was promised to Abraham's children, grandchildren, and the generations that have followed belongs to you also! Welcome to the family! Now, receive the blessing of Abraham, your rightful inheritance in Christ.

That means all of Abraham's children, his descendants, are in line to receive you—and we are also in direct line to receive! That means everything I have been talking about in this book, the same breath of the Spirit of God, that fifth letter of the Hebrew alphabet (hey) and all that goes along with it, is yours today to experience by faith because the blood decrees it.

Need a little more assurance that this blessing of Abraham is really for you? Then read on a little further in Galatians 3: *"So then they which be of faith are blessed with faithful Abraham"* (Galatians 3:9 KJV). Not only are you a child of Abraham, but the Word says here clearly that you are blessed *with* faithful Abraham; in other words, you receive the same blessing he did.

Look at what Paul says in Galatians 3:13-14 (NKJV): *"Christ has redeemed us from the curse of the law, having become a curse for us (for it is written, 'Cursed is everyone who hangs on a tree'), that the blessing of Abraham might come upon the Gentiles in Christ Jesus, that we might receive the promise of the Spirit through faith."*

Galatians 3:13 clearly states that Christ has redeemed us from the curse of the law. Let's stop right there and establish this fact: if you are a Christian and have been redeemed by the blood of Jesus, you are not cursed! You are blessed! The blood of Jesus forever lifted the curse that was introduced into the world through the fall of Adam and Eve because Jesus, the second Adam, paid the penalty and price for us to be free of the curse.

Regardless of your past, whether you were involved in the occult, witchcraft or any of the like, no matter what you have done or how bad you have been, know that now that you are in Christ those demonic spirits no longer have authority or dominion over you and you are free from their control by the blood of Jesus! That is why I can say boldly, *you are not cursed, you are blessed!*

"That the blessing of Abraham might come upon the Gentiles [you and me] in Christ Jesus; that we might receive the promise of the Spirit through faith" (Galatians 3:14 NKJV). Did you notice that verse 14 begins with the word *that*, which is a connector between verse 13 and verse 14. In other words, Christ did all that He did in verse 13 (took the curse and penalty of sin and sickness for us) so *"that the blessing of Abraham might come upon the Gentiles...."* Stop! That means you! That means me! Even though we are not Abraham's descendants by blood, we still are his children because of the work

of Jesus on the Cross—that is what this verse is saying. The word that should make you shout out in praise realizing all that is yours as a child of Abraham!

But Paul goes even further so there would be absolutely no confusion about what the blessing is and defines it in the latter part of verse 14 when he says it's *"the promise of the Spirit through faith!"* What is the blessing of Abraham? Say it with me, please: "It's the promise of the Spirit through faith!" One more time so that it sinks deep into your spirit: *the blessing of Abraham is the promise of the Spirit through faith!* It couldn't be any clearer than that—but sadly, many of us, including myself, have not fully grasped what the apostle Paul was trying to tell us here in Galatians. The blessing was passed to you and me as believers by the Spirit of Grace, the "hey" of the Spirit through the Cross, and we are now recipients by faith in Christ Jesus! Wow! What a glorious thought! What a marvelous inheritance is ours! The blood decrees so!

DECREE

Today, because the blood decrees so, I am an inheritor of the blessings of Abraham, the promise of the Spirit through faith. The same life-giving breath of God that breathed into old Abram and Sarai's bodies and brought about miraculous power, is breathing in me. Dead things come to life in Jesus' name by the breath of the Spirit. I take my inheritance, and I receive all the blessings that Christ purchased for me and was transferred to me through the Cross of Christ because His blood says so!

SIXTEEN

The Blood Decrees Grace

The letter and word *hey*, the Hebrew letter that God inserted into Abram's name making him Abraham, also means "the Spirit of Grace." Grace is the conduit through which all blessing from the Lord comes to us. Apart from the grace of God, we could never experience all that the Lord purchased for us on Calvary. It is by grace that all the blessings that Christ purchased for us with His blood come to us. Only His infinite and amazing grace qualifies us to receive that favor from God and is simply to be received, not earned or worked for. When God breathes on your life with that divine breath, it comes with supernatural favor and blessing. Throughout the Bible, the number 5 is referred to as the number of Grace.

One of the strongest proofs of this is the fact that as mentioned earlier, this word *hey* is the fifth letter of the Hebrew alphabet, but there are many more examples throughout the Word of God.

We often use the words grace and mercy interchangeably, but they are somewhat different in meaning. I have heard it said that "Mercy means we DON'T get what we DO deserve!" What don't we get because of the mercy of the Lord? We don't get condemnation, shame, judgment, punishment, failure, loss, poverty, and even death.

However, I've also heard it said that grace means just the reverse, "Grace means I DO get what I DON"T deserve!" What DO we get that we DON'T deserve because of God's infinite grace toward us? Instead of punishment, judgment, shame, and even death, because of God's amazing love for us and through His grace, we get what we don't deserve such as forgiveness, no condemnation, protection, favor, righteousness, peace, and the blessing of hope and all of these *better things* that Hebrews 12:24 declares the blood decrees plus a future eternally with Christ Jesus.

It is by grace that all the blessings Christ purchased for us with His blood and that His blood decrees come to us. Today we are grateful for both His abundant mercy and grace coming to us all by the blessing of the Spirit of Grace living and breathing in us!

The story recorded for us in Zechariah 4 brings further revelation to the fact that when the Spirit of Grace breathes in your direction, miraculous things can and will happen. The prophet Zechariah spoke this mighty Word of the Lord to a man by the name of Zerubbabel. Zerubbabel oversaw rebuilding the city of Jerusalem after their long captivity in Babylon. As happens to all of us at times, Zerubbabel became discouraged because he was receiving opposition from the surrounding countries, which was preventing him from accomplishing the work of the Lord.

The enemy of our soul hates the work of God and hates the man or woman of God who tries to accomplish it. He will do everything he can to bring discouragement and confusion to try and prevent it from being successful. That is why we must stay focused on the Word of the Lord that gives us the strength to carry on and persist, no matter what obstacle may be standing in our way!

So God sent the prophet Zechariah to Zerubbabel to encourage him. God always has the right Word for us in our time of need!

Zechariah, under the inspiration of the Spirit of the Lord, speaks these well-known words to him: *"'Not by might, nor by power, but by my Spirit,' says the Lord Almighty"* (Zechariah 4:6 NIV). He was telling Zerubbabel to stop trying to make it happen in his own strength, ability, intellect, and even financial means, and let God do it. He was saying, "I can accomplish in one divine moment what cannot be made to happen in hours, days, weeks, months, and even years in the natural." He tells him to prophesy *to* the mountain and challenge its authority. Zechariah 4:7 says, *"Who are you, O great mountain"* standing in the way of Zerubbabel? Sometimes you not only have to speak to God about the mountain or Goliath (giant) standing in your way, you have to actually *speak to the mountain or Goliath* and say, "Who do you think you are standing in the way of Lord!" When God's Spirit of grace comes upon you like it did Zerubbabel, it will cause miraculous things to happen!

Also in Zechariah 4:7 (KJV), we discover what would prophetically be the outcome when he (Zerubbabel) obeyed the word of the Lord and spoke to the mountain: *"thou shalt become a plain* [the problem likened to a mountain standing before him and blocking his success or achievement]: *and he shall bring forth the headstone thereof with shoutings, crying, Grace, grace unto it."* The prophet Zechariah assured Zerubbabel that when he did what the Spirit of the Lord was telling him to do, the result would be a divine and supernatural intervention by God in the situation, and God would cause him to be successful in completing the task he was called to do to bring about a victory.

GRACE, GRACE

Notice it says, *"he shall bring forth the headstone."* The headstone was the very last stone to be put in place when construction of an edifice or wall was being built. The placement of the headstone represented symbolically that the work was done, that it had been accomplished. That is why Jesus cried, "It is finished!" because the Bible tells in Ephesians 2:20 that He was the Chief Cornerstone or headstone. In other words, when He cried, "It is finished," or *tetelestai* in the original Greek language of the New Testament, He was saying I have finished the work of salvation and accomplished the will of the Father forever. His blood decreed so!

We can cease from our labors and rest in the finished work of the Lord on Calvary knowing He already took care of whatever it is we are struggling with. He has already provided the grace and power to provide all our need and for every hindering spirit to be defeated. All we need to do is speak, "Grace, grace unto it," and watch the Spirit of the Lord bring it about!

Very often when I minister in a church for the first time, the Holy Spirit will impress on me to call the pastor and his wife, sometimes the entire pastoral team, to come forward. I will then ask the congregation to stretch out their hands toward them and prophetically speak out of their mouths, "Grace, grace to it." You might ask why I do that? The same demons that challenged Zerubbabel's work, the work of the Lord in rebuilding the walls of Jerusalem, are still fighting and opposing the work of the Lord today.

Pastors (and their families) are prime targets for their attacks; and sadly today, we hear instance after instance of pastors leaving the ministry, closing what were once great churches and giving up because they are quite frankly tired of the fight. This should not be, church! This should not happen when God has given us His Spirit of Grace like He did to Zerubbabel and His power to fulfill His divine plan! We, the body of Christ, need to be speaking,

"Grace, grace to it!" and believe that the same Holy Spirit that came on Zerubbabel when He heard the Word of the Lord by the prophet Zechariah, *"'Not by might nor by power, but by My Spirit,' says the Lord of hosts"* (Zechariah 4:6 NKJV), will breathe on our pastors, renewing them, giving them courage and faith to believe and hope, which is the confident expectation of good. I can't tell you how many of the pastors and wives I have done this for have said afterward, "I feel fresh fire, fresh vision, and new life to do the work that the Lord has called me to do!"

Let this story and these powerful words be an encouragement to you right now as I speak them over your life through the pages of this book under the anointing of the Holy Spirit. "Grace to it! Man or woman of God, the breath of the Holy Spirit breathes in you right now to quicken you and empower you with His divine grace, ability and power to accomplish what He has called you do in the name of Jesus!"

I not only do this for the pastors and staff, but I will often have the members of the congregation think of that need, that obstacle to their faith, that physical or emotional problem, that relationship issue, that financial bondage, and tell them to place their hands on their heart and to speak, "Grace, grace to it!" As they speak these words, I encourage them to believe that the same Spirit of the Lord who breathed into father Abraham is breathing His abundant grace into them, their situations, their needs, and will bring about the victory for them in the name of the Lord of hosts, the name of Jesus! Praise God! Many have received their healing right then and there because of this exercise in faith.

Many times throughout the years of travel and ministry I have wondered, *Will I have the strength to make it through the many services and hours of ministry ahead of me?* And God has poured out

His immeasurable grace just when I needed it and enabled me to minister in His name.

What are you facing today? What is standing in your way of divine health? What situation has come against your finances or your family life or your business or your marriage? I challenge you to pray in the Spirit and then do as the prophet Zechariah instructed Zerubbabel to do, speak, "Grace, grace to it," and watch God intervene and bring about your miracle.

In fact, as you're reading this, I'm praying this over you right now. Note though, Zerubbabel's prayer was "after" the Spirit of the Lord came on him, which made his prayer more than just words spoken out of his mouth but elevated it to the prophetic or supernatural realm. Spend some time in God's holy presence through worship and prayer, letting Him breathe on your heart and into your spirit His quickening prayer, and then pray this prayer and watch God's Spirit bring it about as you speak, "Grace, grace to it!" He will bring you into agreement with what the blood decrees.

His very essence, His nature, is grace. He, the Holy Spirit, is the Divine Executor of the Father's will, recorded for us in the Word and paid for by the blood of Jesus, the Son of God who speaks. I like to say it this way: the Word of God is the Living Will of the Father, paid for by the Son and made available to us through the Spirit, the Spirit of Grace. The heavenly contract was signed by the precious blood of Jesus when He died for us on the Cross.

Not reading the Word of God or studying the Scriptures to discover all that is ours in Christ is like the children of a rich man not bothering to attend the reading of his will and thereby never knowing and forfeiting what their father's intention was for them. As a last will and testament of an earthly man or woman in a sense speaks from the grave their wishes for their loved ones, so the blood of Jesus speaks to us eternally of the will of God for us, His children, and our divine inheritance as believers and children of the Most High (Hebrews 12:24).

Ruth, Naomi, and Boaz

When thinking about the subject of grace and where it is depicted in the Bible, the beautiful story of Ruth and the favor she experienced is, in my opinion, a perfect picture of the grace of the Lord. Just as He orchestrated the steps of Ruth's life, so God will position us for divine favor and redeem our lives from what may seemingly be devastating or dead-end circumstances, if we allow His Holy Spirit to do so!

Ruth was from the country of Moab and was the daughter-in-law of Naomi, who was an Israelite from the city of Bethlehem. Naomi's husband, Elimelech, had moved the family from Bethlehem during a drought to Moab to provide for his family. After several years there, Naomi's husband died, and eventually her two sons, Mahlon and Chilion, married Moabite women: Orpah and Ruth. Sadly, Naomi's two sons also died about ten years later, leaving their wives, Ruth and Orpah, as widows along with their mother-in-law, Naomi.

After their deaths, Naomi heard that the Lord had restored the land of her birth, Israel, with food and abundance so she decided to return home. She told her two daughters-in-law to go back to their families, blessed them, and said good-bye. Orpah decided to return to her people, but Ruth pledged to stay with her mother-in-law, Naomi, and the two of them returned to Israel. The divine decision that Ruth made set in motion a literal and spiritual harvest in not only her life but in the generations to follow, including you and me!

Upon returning to Israel, they found themselves in a destitute position without food or provision of any kind. Little did they know that God was about to shower them with His grace and favor and completely turn their lives around, restoring to them more than what they had lost.

Location, location, location is a phrase we hear often with regard to whether a business will be successful, or a property will increase in value. It's also true in the spiritual realm. Our harvest, our season of recovery, is often connected to our location—not just our geographical location but our location in proximity to the heart of God. Ruth 1:22 (NKJV) says, speaking of Naomi, Ruth's mother-in-law, *"...they came to Bethlehem in the beginning of barley harvest."* The decision to move to back to Bethlehem triggered a harvest for Naomi, Ruth, and her entire family.

It so "happened" that Naomi's husband, Elimelech, had a kinsman who was a man of great wealth; his name was Boaz. Boaz, in Scripture, is a type or foreshadow of Jesus, our Kinsman-Redeemer who has shown us His grace (favor) and desires to bless us. You will see this clearly as I continue to describe for you the events that happened next in this amazing story of grace and favor!

Ruth says to Naomi in Ruth 2:2 (NIV): *"Let me go to the fields and pick up the leftover grain behind anyone in whose eyes I find favor."* The King James version uses the word *grace* in place of the word *favor.*

Now watch this, Ruth didn't realize it, but of all the fields that she could have chosen to go and glean corn, she "happens" to pick the one belonging to Boaz, Naomi's kinsman. By divine providence, she was led to that field to be positioned for favor. As the story goes, Boaz, who again, is a type of Christ in the Bible, a picture of our kinsman in that Jesus came to earth in the form of a human like us, takes note of Ruth and decides to show her favor.

Have you ever felt unappreciated or that your loyalty has been overlooked? Ruth could have felt that way, but as it turned out, someone was taking note of it all along and rewarded her with great favor. Ruth 2:11 (NIV) says, *"Boaz* [a type of Christ] *replied, I've been told all about what you have done for your mother-in-law since the death of your husband...."* In verse 12 Boaz continues to speak, saying, *"May the Lord repay you for what you have done. May you be richly rewarded by the Lord...under whose wings you have come to take refuge."* Ruth's faithfulness and loyalty triggered a harvest of favor from Boaz that became the salvation of her entire family. Even though you may feel overlooked, remember the Lord is watching! He will reward your faithfulness with great favor!

Boaz instructs his workers to let *"grain from the bundles fall purposely"* so that Ruth can glean them and have enough food to take home for her and Naomi. In fact, Boaz tells Ruth not to go anywhere else to glean, only his field. He warns his workers not to reproach or rebuke her.

Ruth is amazed at the favor she has been shown by this man Boaz and goes home to tell Naomi about it, bringing the sheaves of grain he has so graciously allowed her to glean. After inquiring about where Ruth had gleaned, Naomi realizes that this man is the kinsmen of her late husband and that the Lord God of Israel is surely in this encounter.

A word about the culture in that day is helpful here. When a man died without children or heirs, it was necessary that a family member not only purchase or redeem the property that formerly belonged to the deceased man and his wife, but also to marry her to carry on the name of the deceased. In this case, Naomi's husband, Elimelech, was deceased as well as his sons, one of which was Ruth's husband. Word would go around about the situation, and the next in line by relation was to step up and honor the dead. If the next in line was not able to marry the widow, then the process would proceed until an appropriate husband was found.

Naomi, being aware of this culture, instructed Ruth to go back in the evening after the day's work is done, after Boaz has had his evening meal and has laid down to rest. She told her to lift his skirt—in those days men wore long garments that went down to their feet—and lay there until morning. As mentioned in "The Blood Decrees Protection" chapter, the powerful symbolism in this gesture is a perfect picture of Christ, our Kinsmen-Redeemer, covering us with His precious blood when we lay down our lives at His feet.

When Boaz awoke and discovered her there, lying at his feet, he knew that she was a virtuous woman, and in keeping with the cultural mandate, he went to the gate of the city (where all business transaction took place in those days) to inquire if there was a legitimate next of kin to marry Ruth. He meets the man who is next in line as a kinsmen there at the gate and explains the situation. However, this man was not able to marry Ruth, so this cleared Boaz to do so.

Boaz takes Ruth as his wife and soon she bears him a son. Do you see the picture of Christ purchasing us, the church, His bride, and making us part of his family here? Naomi, Ruth's mother-in-law, becomes the nurse for the child and in her old age, Her family is restored once again. In fact, the women of the village said:

> Blessed be the Lord, who has not left you this day without a close relative [kinsman].... And may he [prophetically speaking of Christ] be to you a restorer of life and a nourisher of your old age; for your daughter-in- law, who loves you, who is better to you than seven sons, has borne him (Ruth 4:14-15 NKJV).

The presence of Christ by His Holy Spirit in your life causes Him to be the restorer of life! When God's blessing of grace and favor are breathed into your life, He redeems the past, its mistakes and failures, its shattered pieces and broken dreams, and restores your life to the abundant life that God originally intended for you and me.

I believe He will also not only give you more years or extend your life but will also cause those years to be quality years, for the Word says of Him, *"Who satisfies your mouth with good things, so that your youth is renewed like the eagle's"* (Psalm 103:5 NKJV). An eagle's beak and feathers continually replenish themselves throughout the course of its lifetime, which would be why the Scripture refers to their youth being renewed.

Remember, the Holy Spirit who lives within us when we accept Christ as our Savior, our Kinsmen-Redeemer, is the Spirit of Grace. His presence in your life will cause them to say of you what they said of Naomi: *Blessed be the Lord who has not left you this day without a kinsman*...and they will know that *He is the restorer of life and a nourisher in your old age* (see Ruth 4:14-15).

Ruth found her deliverance, her life restoration, incredible grace, and favor in the presence of her kinsman-redeemer, Boaz. Boaz in Scripture is a type or shadow of our Lord Jesus Christ, our Kinsman-Redeemer. In His presence grace flows into our lives the same way it did into this amazing woman's life, Ruth.

There's an amazing verse in Habakkuk 3:4 (AMP) that underscores this powerful truth: *"His brightness is like the sunlight; He has [bright] rays flashing from His hand, and there [in the sunlike splendor] is the hiding place of His power."* Notice, God's power is hidden in His presence! His radiance is the reflected glory of God, His presence. When your spirit feels the warmth of His radiant or Shekinah glory, you are divinely connected to a heavenly source of power—resurrection power. The result is an outpouring of grace—grace for miracles, grace for deliverance, grace for reconciliation, grace for provision, and so much more! This is all yours and mine as part of what the blood decrees over us. All of this is ours because the blood says so!

CONCLUSION

As I close this book about how the blood of Jesus decrees, that it speaks "better things," and that the blood of Jesus is decreeing and speaking still today, I pray that it has in some way opened your eyes to see all that is being spoken over you by the blood of Jesus right now! That it has birthed a desire in you to go after all the better things that the blood decrees and not allow the enemy to rob you of them any longer.

We know that the Word of God clearly states that *"in the last days, perilous times will come"* (2 Timothy 3:1 NKJV). Those who know what the blood decrees will be immune from fear and realize that we indeed *"are seated in heavenly places with Christ Jesus"* far above any demonic principality or power (Ephesians 2:6).

In closing, allow me to reiterate the *better things* that the blood decrees—and in faith I encourage you to respond out loud: ***"the blood says so!"***

- I am the redeemed of the Lord and I say so! I am a new creation in Christ Jesus; old things have passed away, and all things have become new! My heart has been stamped with His signet ring, and I now bear His image. Because...
- I am the righteousness of God in Christ because He who knew no sin, became sin for me and now I am made the righteousness of Christ in Him! Because...

- I have been reconciled to the Father through the Son and there is no more separation between us. I now enjoy the uninterrupted presence of God. I have been restored to fellowship with God and I have access to His throne of grace continually! Because…
- Your Word, Lord, says that *"with Your stripes we are healed."* I believe Your Word and that those stripes speak healing to my body today in the name of Jesus, the Lord who heals. I take my healing physically, spiritually, emotionally, and mentally and all aspects that concern my life. You are the Lord who heals; Your Word says so and I agree with Your Word. Because…
- The Breaker, the Messiah, sets me free and whomever the Son sets free is free indeed! No bondage or chains can keep me bound because the power of His blood is stronger! Because….
- I take my seat at the King's table knowing that You care for me, and You will supply all my needs according to Your riches in glory by Christ Jesus. Because…
- I refuse to allow my heart to be troubled. I receive Your perfect peace today, which is my inheritance in Christ. Because…
- I thank You, God, that just like David, I recover all that has been stolen from me. You are my Restorer, my Kinsman-Redeemer. Because…
- Today, Your blood speaks protection over me and my family. Just as You protected the children of Israel and the evil passed over them, You will continue to do the same for me and my house. Because…
- Your Word declares I overcome by the blood of the Lamb and by the word of my testimony. I testify in agreement with Your Word and with what Your blood decrees. Because…

- Today, I walk by faith in what Your blood speaks, Jesus! I receive it as my inheritance as a child of Abraham. That same unwavering faith is mine today and I believe Your Word. Because…
- I am a child of Abraham and the recipient of His blessing. The same breath of the Spirit that quickened his aged body is breathing in me, making dead things come to life. Because…
- I receive the grace of the Spirit of the Lord for every facet of my being. I walk in His favor and know that He prepares a table before me in the presence of my enemies. Because…

Allow me pray this blessing over you in closing:

Father, we know that every word of Scripture is God-breathed and recorded for our benefit; so right now we speak, "Grace, grace to it," to whatever has become an obstacle in the way of my dear friend who is reading this book. If this reader has never come to know Jesus as Redeemer, Lord, reveal Yourself and make this person a new creation in You today.

Breathe grace to their body and healing, in the name of Jesus. Grace to their marriage which may be at an impasse and may seem there's no hope of being healed. Grace to their finances and the bank account that never seems to have enough. Grace to the child who is away from the Lord or involved in drugs or in rebellion—grace to bring about divine reconciliation and restoration of faith. Grace! Grace to it! Be healed, delivered, breathed on by the Spirit of the Lord because the blood decrees it!

Cause this precious reader to declare what the blood decrees is theirs in Christ Jesus. To realize that the blood speaks redemption, righteousness, reconciliation, and access to the throne of grace, restoration and recovery, healing, deliverance, a seat at the Lord's table, protection, overcoming power, peace, abundance, the blessing of Abraham, grace and faith to believe like Abraham, because *the blood says so!*

About Jim Cernero

Jim Cernero is a pastor, revivalist, healing and worship minister, composer, and author. By God's grace, through his ministry over the past 45-plus years, many have come to know the Lord personally as their Savior and Lord; many have been discipled and have come into maturity spiritually; many have been healed by the power of God from various diseases! Schedule permitting and Lord willing, Jim would love to come and minister at your church or conference as the Holy Spirit leads.

* * *

If you'd like to invite Pastor Jim to speak at your church or conference, please email him at: certainsoundchurchintl@outlook.com

If you live in the Austin, Texas, area or are visiting the area, we invite you to visit Certain Sound Church International to worship with us. We meet at:

Film Alley Theater / Theater # 6
420 Wolf Ranch Parkway
Georgetown, TX 78629

Contact Information

Pastors Jim & Mindy Cernero
certainsoundchurchintl.com
Jimcernero.org
Facebook.com/jimcernero

In the Right Hands, This Book Will Change Lives!

Most of the people who need this message will not be looking for this book. To change their lives, you need to **put a copy of this book in their hands.**

Our ministry is constantly seeking methods to find the people who need this anointed message to change their lives. **Will you help us reach these people?**

Extend this ministry by sowing three, five, ten, or *even more* books today and change people's lives for the better! Your generosity will be part of catalyzing the Great Awakening that many have been prophesying and praying for.

From

Ginger Ziegler

YOUR VICTORY—THE DEVIL'S DEFEAT!

Unseen forces and hindrances—fear, failure, sickness, trauma, guilt, and more—often try to stand in your way. These destructive enemies play keep-away with God's best for your life.

Is there a way to permanently overcome? *Yes!* **The Blood of Jesus.**

In *His Blood Speaks*, a powerful 31-day devotional, Ginger Ziegler points out that your victory is in the Voice of Jesus' Blood. When Cain killed his brother, Abel, his blood spoke from the ground, crying vengeance. Today, Jesus' Blood speaks from heaven, crying forgiveness and mercy. As you digest these daily teachings, the Blood will cry on your behalf:

- freedom *not* bondage
- health *not* sickness
- prosperity *not* poverty
- acceptance *not* rejection
- righteousness *not* unrighteousness
- exoneration *not* condemnation
- and everything else you'll ever need

The Blood of Jesus is your major weapon to live victoriously and guarantee the devil's defeat. Start right now living your life in the freedom Jesus' Blood purchased for *you!*

Purchase your copy wherever books are sold